Development Cooperation

DOI: 10.1057/9781137397881.0001

Other Palgrave Pivot titles

Mia Moody-Ramirez and Jannette Dates: The Obamas and Mass Media: Race, Gender, Religion, and Politics

Kenneth Weisbrode: Old Diplomacy Revisited

Christopher Mitchell: Decentralization and Party Politics in the Dominican Republic

Keely Byars-Nichols: The Black Indian in American Literature

Vincent P. Barabba: Business Strategies for a Messy World: Tools for Systemic Problem-Solving

Cristina Archetti: Politicians, Personal Image and the Construction of Political Identity: A Comparative Study of the UK and Italy

Mitchell Congram, Peter Bell and Mark Lauchs: Policing Transnational Organised Crime and Corruption: Exploring Communication Interception Technology

János Kelemen: The Rationalism of Georg Lukács

Patrick Manning: Big Data in History

Susan D. Rose: Challenging Global Gender Violence: The Global Clothesline Project

Thomas Janoski: Dominant Divisions of Labor: Models of Production That Have Transformed the World of Work

Gray Read: Modern Architecture in Theater: The Experiments of Art et Action

Bill Lucarelli: Endgame for the Euro: A Critical Theory

Robert Frodeman: Sustainable Knowledge: A Theory of Interdisciplinarity

Antonio V. Menéndez Alarcón: French and US Approaches to Foreign Policy

Stephen Turner: American Sociology: From Pre-Disciplinary to Post-Normal

Ekaterina Dorodnykh: Stock Market Integration: An International Perspective

Mercedes Bunz: The Silent Revolution: How Digitalization Transforms Knowledge, Work, Journalism and Politics without Making Too Much Noise

Kishan S. Rana: The Contemporary Embassy: Paths to Diplomatic Excellence

Mark Bracher: Educating for Cosmopolitanism: Lessons from Cognitive Science and Literature

Carroll P. Kakel, III: The Holocaust as Colonial Genocide: Hitler's 'Indian Wars' in the 'Wild East'

Laura Linker: Lucretian Thought in Late Stuart England: Debates about the Nature of the Soul

Nicholas Birns: Barbarian Memory: The Legacy of Early Medieval History in Early Modern Literature

Adam Graycar and Tim Prenzler: Understanding and Preventing Corruption

Michael J. Pisani: Consumption, Informal Markets, and the Underground Economy: Hispanic Consumption in South Texas

DOI: 10.1057/9781137397881.0001

palgrave▸**pivot**

Development Cooperation: Challenges of the New Aid Architecture

Stephan Klingebiel

Head of Bi- and Multilateral Development Cooperation, German Development Institute

DOI: 10.1057/9781137397881.0001

First published 2014 by
PALGRAVE MACMILLAN

Palgrave Macmillan in the UK is an imprint of Macmillan Publishers Limited, registered in England, company number 785998, of Houndmills, Basingstoke, Hampshire RG21 6XS.

Palgrave Macmillan in the US is a division of St Martin's Press LLC, 175 Fifth Avenue, New York, NY 10010.

Palgrave Macmillan is the global academic imprint of the above companies and has companies and representatives throughout the world.

Palgrave® and Macmillan® are registered trademarks in the United States, the United Kingdom, Europe and other countries.

ISBN: 978–1–137–39789–8 EPUB
ISBN: 978–1–137–39788–1 PDF
ISBN: 978–1–137–39787–4 Hardback

A catalogue record for this book is available from the British Library.

A catalog record for this book is available from the Library of Congress.

www.palgrave.com/pivot

DOI: 10.1057/9781137397881

Contents

DOI: 10.1057/9781137397881.0001

List of Figures

▶

List of Tables

DOI: 10.1057/9781137397881.0003

List of Boxes

DOI: 10.1057/9781137397881.0004

Acknowledgements

The author would like to thank the following organisations for permission to reproduce copyright material:

Organisation for Economic Co-operation and Development (OECD) for: OECD (2011) Aid Effectiveness 2005–10: Progress in Implementing the Paris Declaration http://www.oecd.org/dac/effectiveness/48742718.pdf.

and

OECD DAC List of ODA Recipients Effective for reporting on 2012 and 2013 flows http://www.oecd.org/dac/stats/DAC%20List%20used%20for%202012%20and%202013%20flows.pdf.

United Nations (UN) for MDG Monitor Tracking the Millennium Development Goals: browse by goal http://www.mdgmonitor.org/browse_goal.cfm.

DOI: 10.1057/9781137397881.0005

List of Abbreviations

AwZ	Ausschuss für wirtschaftliche Zusammenarbeit und Entwicklung (Committee for Economic Cooperation and Development)
BMZ	Bundesministerium für wirtschaftliche Zusammenarbeit und Entwicklung (German Ministry for Economic Cooperation and Development)
BMGF	Bill and Melinda Gates Foundation
CDI	Commitment to Development Index
CGD	Centre for Global Development
CPA	Country Programmable Aid
DAC	Development Assistance Committee
DEG	Deutsche Investitions-und Entwicklungsgesellschaft (German Investment and Development Company)
DFID	Department for International Development
EAC	East African Community
EDF	European Development Fund
EU	European Union
FC	financial cooperation
FDI	foreign direct investment
G8	Group of Eight
G20	Group of Twenty
GDP	gross domestic product
GDR	German Democratic Republic
GIZ	Deutsche Gesellschaft für Internationale Zusammenarbeit (German International Cooperation Agency)
GNI	gross national income

GPG	global public goods
GTZ	Deutsche Gesellschaft für Technische Zusammenarbeit (German Technical Cooperation Agency)
HIPC	heavily indebted poor country
HIV	human immunodeficiency virus
IMF	International Monetary Fund
KfW	Kreditanstalt für Wiederaufbau (Reconstruction Credit Institute; German government-owned development bank)
LDC	least developed country
LIC	low-income country
MDGs	Millennium Development Goals
M&E	monitoring and evaluation
MIC	middle-income country
NGO	non-governmental organisation
OBA	output-based aid
ODA	Official Development Assistance
OECD	Organisation for Economic Co-operation and Development
P4P	Pay for Performance
PFM	public financial management
RBA	results-based aid
RBF	results-based financing
SADC	Southern African Development Community
SDGs	Sustainable Development Goals
TC	technical cooperation
UN	United Nations
UNDP	United Nations Development Programme

DOI: 10.1057/9781137397881.0006

1
What Is Development Cooperation?

Abstract: *Development cooperation is a comparatively new concept in international relations, having risen in importance only after the Second World War. The aims of and motives for development cooperation have since changed significantly. Besides pursuing short- and longer-term objectives in their own economic, foreign policy and other interests, donors usually have a recognisable and genuine interest in assisting countries in their processes of development. In the Millennium Development Goals (MDGs), the international community has an acknowledged frame of reference for global objectives, which play a major role not least in development cooperation.*

Klingebiel, Stephan. *Development Cooperation: Challenges of the New Aid Architecture.* Basingstoke: Palgrave Macmillan, 2014. DOI: 10.1057/9781137397881.0007.

1.1   Definitions, distinctions and scale

1.1.1   Definition

Development cooperation is generally understood to serve the purpose of assisting countries in their efforts to make social and economic progress. But is every form of cooperation with developing countries to be regarded as development cooperation? Who, in fact, determines whether a country is a developing country in the first place? What forms of cooperation should be seen as aid? Does military aid not help the recipient country too? What about commercial forms of cooperation; are they also to be seen as development cooperation? Should new forms of cooperation – as between China and African countries – also be regarded as forms of development cooperation?

Donors of development aid have agreed to lay down rules, especially within the framework of the Organisation for Economic Co-operation and Development (OECD), which has its own development committee, the Development Assistance Committee (DAC), mandated with tasks associated with development cooperation, known internationally as Official Development Assistance (ODA). The OECD considers not only appropriate standards for development cooperation, but also what distinguishes it from other areas. It is examining, for example, standards concerning forms of export subsidisation that may distort and obstruct competition. The interface between "development cooperation" on the one hand and, say, "unwanted distortion of competition" (due to export subsidies, for instance) on the other thus forms part of the debates on development cooperation arrangements.

The OECD's Development Assistance Committee has agreed that the following criteria[1] must be met if international assistance is to be recognised as development cooperation:

▸ The assistance must be provided for *developing countries*. There is a list of developing countries, which is updated every three years. It is essentially based on the commonly used well-being indicator "per capita income" (gross national income – GNI – per capita of the population) and distinguishes between the poorest and other poor countries and two groups of middle-income countries.

  Although it is relatively clear to which category most countries belong, there are always doubtful cases. Qatar, Singapore (both until 1996), Hong Kong (until 1997) and Saudi Arabia (until 2008), for example, stayed on the list of developing countries for a long time. Some of today's "donors", such as Portugal, Greece and South Korea, were formerly on the "list of recipients". In all, far more countries have been removed from the "list of recipients" (35) since 1970 than have been added to it (15; partly because of the collapse of the Soviet Union) (see, OECD/DAC 2011b).

▸ The assistance must be conducive to *economic development* or the *improvement of living standards*. Although this goal is somewhat vague, it clearly indicates that the definition does not extend, for example, to military assistance or to the supply of luxury goods to an upper stratum of society.

▸ The assistance must consist of *grants* or *concessional loans*. While grants are seen as pure donations (not to be repaid in any way), loans must contain what is known as a grant element of at least 25 per cent. The grant element is arrived at from the degree of concession (with due regard for the loan period and the interest rate) compared to a commercial loan.

Definitions are often difficult and politically sensitive in the development cooperation context. Time and again there are, for example, debates on why participation in UN peace-keeping missions in developing countries does not come under the heading of development cooperation (the costs have not hitherto been attributable to ODA) or why certain expenditure on accommodation for refugees in a donor country can sometimes be regarded as development cooperation.

Donors are very interested in there being a uniform definition of development cooperation because it will enable them to compare the various forms of assistance provided. International agreements reached under the United Nations' auspices and political commitments by the eight leading industrialised countries (G8) have again and again helped to bring political pressure on the wealthy states to provide more development aid. As early as 1970 agreement was reached on the still controversial (non-binding) target set for the industrialised countries of devoting 0.7 per cent of their gross national income to development cooperation. Donors therefore have an interest in seeing as much as possible of their assistance recorded in international development cooperation statistics.

DOI: 10.1057/9781137397881.0007

TABLE 1.1 *DAC list of ODA recipients*

Least Developed Countries	Other Low Income Countries (per capita GNI <= \$1 005 in 2010)	Lower Middle Income Countries and Territories (per capita GNI \$1 006–\$3 975 in 2010)	Upper Middle Income Countries and Territories (per capita GNI \$3 976–\$12 275 in 2010)
Afghanistan	Kenya	Armenia	Albania
Angola	Korea, Dem. Rep.	Belize	Algeria
Bangladesh	Kyrgyz Rep.	Bolivia	*Anguilla
Benin	Tajikistan	Cameroon	Antigua and Barbuda
Bhutan	Zimbabwe	Cape Verde	Argentina
Burkina Faso		Congo, Rep.	Azerbaijan
Burundi		Côte d'Ivoire	Belarus
Cambodia		Egypt	Bosnia and Herzegovina
Central African Rep.		El Salvador	Botswana
Chad		Fiji	Brazil
Comoros		Georgia	Chile
Congo, Dem. Rep.		Ghana	China
Djibouti		Guatemala	Colombia
Equatorial Guinea		Guyana	Cook Islands
Eritrea		Honduras	Costa Rica
Ethiopia		India	Cuba
Gambia		Indonesia	Dominica
Guinea		Iraq	Dominican Republic
Guinea-Bissan		Kosovo¹	Ecuador
Haiti		Marshall Islands	Former Yugoslav Republic
Kiribati		Micronesia, Federated States	of Macedonia
Laos		Moldova	Gabon
Lesotho		Mongolia	Grenada
Liberia		Morocco	Iran
Madagascar		Nicaragua	Jamaica
Malawi		Nigeria	Jordan
Mali		Pakistan	Kazakhstan
Mauritania		Papua New Guinea	Lebanon
Mozambique		Paraguay	Libya
Myanmar		Philippines	Malaysia
Nepal		Sri Lanka	Maldives
Niger		Swaziland	Mauritius
Rwanda		Syria	Mexico
Samoa		*Tokelau	Montenegro
São Tomé and Príncipe		Tonga	*Montserrat
Senegal		Turkmenistan	Namibia
Sierra Leone		Ukraine	Nauru
Solomon Islands		Uzbekistan	Niue
Somalia		Vietnam	Palau
South Sudan		West Bank ana Gaza Strip	Panama
Sudan			Peru
Tanzania			Serbia
Timor-Leste			Seychelles
Togo			South Africa
Tuvalu			*St. Helena
Uganda			St. Kitts-Nevis
Vanuatu			St. Lucia
Yemen			St. Vincent and Grenadines
Zambia			Suriname
			Thailand
			Tunisia
			Turkey
			uruguay
			Venezuela
			*Wallis and Futuna

Note: * Territory.
¹ This is without prejudice to the status of Kosovo under international law.

Source: OECD (s.a.).

DOI: 10.1057/9781137397881.0007

1.1.2   Scale of development cooperation[2]

There are various ways of determining, describing and assessing the scale of development cooperation. These various perspectives are important when it comes to appraising donors' contributions and the significance of those resources to developing countries. However, the question of "input" is only one relevant facet, since it does not initially say much about the effects achieved.

The donors who make up the OECD's Development Assistance Committee provided a total of US$ 126 billion in 2012, the second year in succession in which the total fell in real terms. Measured against the donors' economic strength, this was equivalent to 0.29 per cent of gross national income.

The USA continues to be the world's largest bilateral donor of development assistance (US$ 30.5 billion or 0.19 per cent ODA/GNI in 2012). It is followed by the United Kingdom (US$ 13.7 billion or 0.56 per cent ODA/GNI), Germany (US$ 13.1 billion or 0.38 per cent ODA/GNI), France (US$ 12.0 billion or 0.45 per cent ODA/GNI) and Japan (US$ 10.5 billion or 0.17 per cent ODA/GNI). In relative terms, however, a number of small and medium-sized donors are far more heavily engaged, this being especially true of Luxembourg, Sweden, Norway, Denmark and the Netherlands, some of which contribute more than 0.7 per cent of their GNI. International non-governmental organisations provide a further amount of well over US$ 15 billion each year.

When all external financial inflows are considered, it is found that private flows have gained significantly on development aid in the longer term and exceeded it in most developing regions. Despite this, development aid continues to be important to the group of the poor and especially the poorest countries for the financing and implementation of poverty and reform programmes. In fragile countries it may be a vital means of counteracting signs of state collapse.

Most of the development assistance provided by donors goes to the countries of sub-Saharan Africa (37.9 per cent in 2010/2011);[3] the proportion has been increased in the past at Asia's expense and takes the comparatively strong economic dynamism of many Asian countries into account. Almost 10 per cent of OECD-DAC development assistance (8.4 per cent in 2011[4]) is available in the form of humanitarian assistance, which is used to alleviate short-term emergency situations.

Over 17 per cent (2010) of aid is provided in (partly) tied form and recorded as such; the provision of aid in these cases is subject to the

DOI: 10.1057/9781137397881.0007

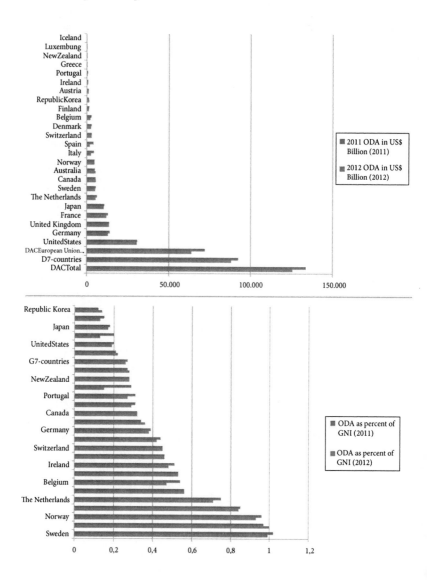

FIGURE 1.1   *Donor performance, 2011–2012*

Source: Author's own compilation, data from: BMZ (2013).

requirement that goods or services are purchased from the donor country. Owing to the absence of international competition, tied aid is more expensive on average and may be of a poorer quality than would result from international calls for tenders. The costs due to the tying of aid are

DOI: 10.1057/9781137397881.0007

some 15 to 30 per cent or, in the case of food aid, as much as some 40 per cent higher than when aid is not tied (Clay et al. 2009, 1). For the sake of development, the abandonment of aid-tying has therefore been demanded for decades. The officially designated instances of aid-tying (as in the case of goods) are joined by other *de facto* tied aid, as in the context of technical assistance, when partner countries are not free to put advisory services out to tender. This practice is similarly criticised as being bad for development (for example, Actionaid 2011; Clay / Geddes / Natali 2009, viii).

In certain circumstances, the cancellation of debts (primarily export credits) may also be recognised as development aid. In the past two decades this step was often an important means of reducing the heavy burden of amortisation and interest payments on the budgets of many developing countries – a problem that remained serious until the late 1990s. Where debt cancellations came in for criticism, it was because they do not make any additional resources available to countries for development purposes, but rather reduce the outflow of resources (for example, Actionaid 2011).

1.1.3   Importance of development cooperation from the developing countries' viewpoint

Development cooperation varies widely in its importance to developing countries. While a group of poor countries continues to be heavily dependent on it, in some respects it now plays no more than a marginal role for other developing countries. Dependence on development cooperation is usually expressed as the ratio of development assistance to a developing country's economic strength (aid/GNI) or as aid in absolute terms per inhabitant of the recipient country (aid per capita). In the first method, the importance of development cooperation largely depends on the country's economic strength. The lower this is, the more likely it is that dependence on aid will be high. Another important question is whether the aid resources are actually "available" to the developing country or "programmable" or consist primarily of statistical variables (as in the case of university fees for students from developing countries).[5]

If all developing countries are considered, the ratio of aid to GNI averages 0.68 per cent (2010).[6] Sub-Saharan Africa, at 4.2 per cent, and Oceania, at 13.2 per cent, are well above this average figure. For certain countries the figure is many times higher, in some cases well above 30 per cent (for example, Burundi: 39.8 per cent, Afghanistan: 34.4 per

DOI: 10.1057/9781137397881.0007

TABLE 1.2 *Net financial flows to developing countries (US$ billions)*

	1990		2000		2010 (provisional estimates)	
	%	US$ bn	%	US$ bn	%	US$ bn
I. All developing countries	100.00	129.0	100.00	274.2	100.00	1,267.2
Thereof:						
(i) Private inflows (thereof: foreign direct investment)	32.1 (16.6)	41.4 (21.4)	0.6 (54.1)	173.8 (148.3)	62.3 (39.9)	790.0 (505.7)
(ii) Public inflows (thereof: development aid)	45.5 (25.7)	58.7 (33.2)	8.2 (10.3)	22.6 (28.3)	12.4 (0.07)	158.3 (89.0)
(iii) Remittances from migrants	22.4	28.9	28.3	77.7	25.1	319.0
II. Middle-income countries (MICs)	100.00	107.0	100.00	252.3	100.00	1,167.0
Thereof:						
(i) Private inflows (thereof: foreign direct investment)	37.9 (19.3)	40.6 (20.7)	67.9 (57.7)	171.4 (145.5)	66.1 (41.9)	772.1 (488.8)
(ii) Public inflows (thereof: development aid)	36.3 (15.9)	38.9 (17.1)	2.9 (0.06)	7.4 (15.4)	8.6 (0.03)	100.7 (39.0)
(iii) Remittances from migrants	25.7 (25.7)	27.5	29.1	73.6	25.2	294.2
III. Low-income countries (LICs)	100.00	22.0	100.00	21.8	100.00	100.2
Thereof:						
(i) Private inflows (thereof: foreign direct investment)	3.6 (0.03)	0.8 (0.7)	11.4 (12.8)	2.5 (2.8)	17.8 (16.9)	17.9 (16.9)
(ii) Public inflows (thereof: development aid)	90 (72.3)	19.8 (15.9)	69.2 (59.1)	15.2 (12.9)	57.4 (49.9)	57.5 (50.0)
(iii) Remittances from migrants	6.4	1.4	18.8	4.1	24.8	24.8

Source: Based on Adugna et al. (2011, 3).

DOI: 10.1057/9781137397881.0007

cent). Aid as a proportion of national budgets in sub-Saharan Africa, for example, is, at over 40 per cent in some countries, high compared to other regions. Statistically, every person in developing countries accounts for US$ 23.5 (2010) of aid annually (the figure for sub-Saharan Africa is US$ 51.1, for Oceania US$ 221.6 and for the Palestinian Territories as much as US$ 607.0).

1.2   Why development aid is provided: motives and interests

Development cooperation is a comparatively new concept in international relations, having risen to significance only after the Second World War (Keely 2012, 68 ff.; Nuscheler 2006, 26 ff.; Ihne / Wilhelm 2006, 6 ff.). Various events and circumstances are of relevance to its emergence: (i) the economic crises and distortions that played a decisive part in political crises between the two world wars were major motivating forces behind the determination to be more active when signs of economic crisis became noticeable; (ii) even while the Second World War was still being fought, it became obvious that the destruction it was causing, particularly in Europe, would necessitate tremendous exertions. The preparations for the establishment of the World Bank, expressly intended for reconstruction, and of the International Monetary Fund and the United Nations system were meant to create appropriate funding opportunities and political fora; (iii) the Marshall Plan set up by the USA in 1948 was similarly designed to help Western Europe overcome the devastation caused by the war. It also reflected the confrontation between the two geopolitical blocs. This situation led to global competition, which found expression not only in Europe but also, and especially, in the regions of the South.

The emergence of development cooperation must therefore be seen essentially as an outcome of the East-West conflict (Nuscheler 2006). The Cold War continued to have an impact on the provision of development assistance in the decades until the Berlin Wall fell. Countries were penalised or rewarded with the prospect of development assistance according to whether they belonged to the western or eastern camp. For the Federal Republic of Germany, policy on the allocation of development aid was at times partly determined by its *Deutschlandpolitik*, its policy on Germany as a whole, in that countries denying the German Democratic

DOI: 10.1057/9781137397881.0007

Republic (GDR), or East Germany, diplomatic recognition were assisted, while development cooperation with countries entering into diplomatic relations with the GDR ceased.

Other donor countries similarly used their development assistance for other foreign policy purposes. For such former colonial powers as France and the United Kingdom, development cooperation was (and, to some extent, continues to be) a means of maintaining special relations with former colonies, most of which gained their independence in the 1960s. Even today many donors allocate a large proportion of development cooperation resources to regions in which they have traditionally had some influence. Belgium, for example, continues to maintain special development relations with its former colonies (Rwanda, Burundi and what is now the Democratic Republic of Congo).

The classical foreign policy motives have been joined by other goals, owing, in particular, to more recent security risks and threats since the East-West conflict came to an end (Klingebiel 2006b). Development cooperation is meant to help stabilise countries and regions where military operations alone are not enough for to ensure a lasting solution to fragility, and efforts need to be made to restore statehood (as in Afghanistan).

Besides foreign and security policy objectives, most donors have an interest in pursuing their own economic goals through development cooperation (Sangmeister / Schönstedt 2010; Nuscheler 2006). The classical goal of gaining and maintaining access to natural resources is again growing in importance because of the increasing scarcity of minerals, oil and so on. A further motive for development cooperation may be a desire to facilitate access to markets, since they can contribute to the development of economic relations. Development cooperation is typically exposed to pressure from a business community wanting a large proportion of the assistance to be spent in the donor country or returned in the form of orders. Such effects can be achieved through aid-tying or other approaches (such as the selection of projects in which businesses in the donor country enjoy competitive advantages) and the award of contracts to domestic consultancies. In development and economic terms, however, they are often to the partner country's disadvantage.

These goals are joined by other motives. Donors have frequently attempted to link development cooperation to migration and asylum issues by associating their willingness to take back deportees with

DOI: 10.1057/9781137397881.0007

development cooperation, for example. In some cases, donors also use development cooperation in their pursuit of long-term global objectives; this is true not least of efforts in the area of climate change. Although this goal is, in principle, shared internationally, a question that arises from the partner countries' point of view is whether the resources actually intended for "national development tasks" should not be used in pursuit of global objectives (such as climate financing) or whether additional sources of finance are needed for this purpose (see, Kaul 2013). This may result in there being more cases of political dispute over the provision of resources for global environmental objectives or national development measures.

Viewed in the long term, development cooperation goals and motives have changed significantly. Besides short- and longer-term objectives in their own interests, most donors can be seen to have a genuine interest in altruistically supporting countries with their development processes. The main aim in this context is to reduce poverty in partner countries.

An indication of a development cooperation policy that is not pre-dominantly geared to the donors' own interests is perhaps the willingness to provide development assistance for poor countries. The development lobby for "altruistic development assistance" that exists in most donor countries is often a force in society that should not be underestimated. Traditionally, the Churches and other civil society groups are engaged in development activities. Non-governmental organisations (NGOs), on the other hand, may well pursue interests of their own, as when it comes to canvassing for funds.

1.3   What is development cooperation meant to achieve?

The Millennium Development Goals

In the Millennium Development Goals (MDGs) the international community has a recognised frame of reference for global objectives. The MDGs were developed at UN level and adopted by the UN member states in 2000. They require, among other things, the halving of the number of people living in extreme poverty by 2015. The eight MDGs include goals in the areas of nutrition, education, health, gender equality, environmental sustainability and the formation of a global partnership for development.

DOI: 10.1057/9781137397881.0007

In developing countries the MDGs often form a basis for governments and donors to agree on joint objectives; they have helped them to set political priorities and have greatly strengthened the consensus on generally recognised objectives (see, ERD 2013). The list of goals has its weaknesses, however. For one thing, they are relatively wide-ranging and ambitious; for another, they do not cover all relevant aspects – good governance, for example, or the preservation of natural resources. Nor do they have much to say on how they are to be achieved or what they mean for individual countries or regions.

Goal 1: Eradicate Extreme Hunger and Poverty | more >>>

Target 1.A : Halve, between 1990 and 2015, the proportion of people whose income is less than one dollar a day

Target 1.B : Achieve full and productive employment and decent work for all, including women and young people

Target 1.C : Halve, between 1990 and 2015, the proportion of people who suffer from hunger

Goal 2: Achieve Universal Primary Education | more >>>

Target 2.A: Ensure that, by 2015, children everywhere, boys and girls alike, will be able to complete a full course of primary schooling

Goal 3: Promote Gender Equality and Empower Women | more >>>

Target 3.A: Eliminate gender disparity in primary and secondary education, preferably by 2005, and in all levels of education no later than 2015

Goal 4: Reduce Child Mortality | more >>>

Target 4.A: Reduce by two-thirds, between 1990 and 2015, the under-five mortality rate

Goal 5: Improve Maternal Health | more >>>

Target 5.A: Reduce by three quarters, between 1990 and 2015, the maternal mortality ratio

FIGURE 1.2   *Continued*

DOI: 10.1057/9781137397881.0007

Goal 6: Combat HIV/AIDS, Malaria and other diseases | more >>>

Target 6.A: Have halted by 2015 and begun to reverse the spread of HIV/AIDS

Target 6.B: Achieve, by 2010, universal access to treatment for HIV/AIDS for all those who need it

Target 6.C: Have halted by 2015 and begun to reverse the incidence of malaria and other major diseases

Goal 7: Ensure Environmental Sustainability | more >>>

Target 7.A: Integrate the principles of sustainable development into country policies and programmes and reverse the loss of environmental resources

Target 7.B: Reduce biodiversity loss, achieving, by 2010, a significant reduction in the rate of loss

Target 7.C: Halve, by 2015, the proportion of people without sustainable access to safe drinking water and basic sanitation

Target 7.D: By 2020, to have achieved a significant improvement in the lives of at least 100 million slum dwellers

Goal 8: Develop a Global Partnership for Development | more >>>

Target 8.A: Develop further an open, rule-based, predictable, non-discriminatory trading and financial system

Target 8.B: Address the special needs of the least developed countries

Target 8.C: Address the special needs of landlocked developing countries and small island developing States (through the Programme of Action for the Sustainable Development of Small Island Developing States and the outcome of the twenty-second special session of the General Assembly)

Target 8.D: Deal comprehensively with the debt problems of developing countries through national and international measures in order to make debt sustainable in the long term

Target 8.E: In cooperation with pharmaceutical companies, provide access to affordable essential drugs in developing countries

Target 8.F: In cooperation with the private sector, make available the benefits of new technologies, especially information and communications

FIGURE 1.2   *The Millennium Development Goals*
Source: MDG monitor (s.a.).

DOI: 10.1057/9781137397881.0007

BOX 1.1   *Sustainability in development cooperation*

Development cooperation is largely determined by the principle of sustainability. The aim of sustainability is permanently viable structures; it precludes a short-term view that neglects the wide-ranging effects that a strategy or project can have. Sustainability is needed at four different levels (see, Heller 2011):

▸ *Budgetary sustainability* requires the long-term financing of projects and strategies. A development cooperation project entailing only the construction of a new vocational school, for example, without the plans (the appropriate budget) taking account of staff wages and salaries and the maintenance of the building, would not be viable from a budgetary point of view and so not sustainable.

▸ *Programmatic sustainability:* Does a contribution of development assistance result in the problem to be solved actually being alleviated? In principle, development cooperation activities can be so planned that they do not make for progress in development that is effective in the long term. The promotion of a new state-owned enterprises, for example, would not be an appropriate means of counteracting supply bottlenecks. It might help to create new problems if it became necessary to subsidise those enterprises in the long term.

▸ *Operational sustainability:* A new hospital in a remote rural area might have difficulty recruiting medical staff if the location was highly unattractive – its operational sustainability would be threatened.

▸ *Ecological sustainability:* If a project harms the natural resource base (through unsuitable felling in a primary forest, for example), ecological sustainability does not prevail.

An agreement to follow the MDGs[7]

Since the autumn of 2012 the first steps towards establishing a new global development agenda have been taken. The aim is to draft an agreement to follow the Millennium Development Goals after 2015. A great deal is still unclear. It remains to be seen, for instance, whether

DOI: 10.1057/9781137397881.0007

a broad consensus of many countries can be achieved or whether a post-MDG document will be backed by no more than a "coalition of the willing". A high-level international panel of advisers has been formed by UN Secretary-General Ban Ki-Moon to draw up proposals for the new development agenda. The panel of advisers is to submit proposals for a new system of goals by the next MDG summit, which is to be held at the time of the UN General Assembly in September 2013.

The disputes over an MDG follow-up agreement vary in nature. Should, for example, the original MDGs simply be improved substantively, or is it time to design a completely new framework? What form should the negotiating process take? Are all countries – the USA, which has been critical of the MDGs, and the emerging economies, for instance – in fact interested in a new development agenda? And with what resources and instruments can new goals be achieved?

Given the likelihood of numerous debates and tough consultations, the important issues need to be enumerated. Three challenges must be taken into account in this process:

1 *Linking the poverty and environment agendas:* Global poverty
   reduction and social progress can be accomplished only if
   development is sustainable and respects planetary limits.
   Recognising this, the Rio+20 summit (in the summer of 2012) set
   up a group of experts to define Sustainable Development Goals
   (SDGs). As so often happens, this has created parallel structures
   within the United Nations. The SDG group's mandate overlaps
   that of the MDG group of experts. Underlying this duplication is
   the conflict between the goals of the traditional poverty reduction
   agenda and those of the sustainable development agenda,
   which dates back to the 1980s. For poverty reduction, economic
   growth and social security systems are necessary, and these are
   associated with increased consumption of natural resources,
   whereas ecological sustainability is geared to respect for planetary
   limits. Such conflicts of objectives are often difficult to resolve.
   Yet there are many avowals and approaches aimed at forging a
   better relationship between sustainable development and poverty
   reduction. This is evident, for example, from the "inclusive green
   growth" initiatives. For the post-2015 negotiations it is therefore
   important that all concerned seize the opportunity to combine the
   two agendas, MDGs and SDGs.

DOI: 10.1057/9781137397881.0007

2   *No worthwhile "global framework" without the emerging economies:*
     Any global agreement must have the backing of a broad consensus.
     For the post-2015 process, then, it is essential that such dynamic
     economies as China, Indonesia and Brazil (together with other
     groups of countries) not only are involved in the processes of
     discussion and negotiation at an early stage, but also play an active
     part in arranging them. Otherwise, a new catalogue of global goals
     will not find sufficient acceptance and will be adopted only with
     difficulty, if at all. The negotiating processes must therefore be open
     to new ideas, concerns and perspectives. As it is still largely unclear
     if the countries in this group actually see the need for a post-2015
     agenda, it is vital for the post-2015 preparations that a dialogue
     (formal consultations, open discussion formats and so on) should
     be established at all levels on the purpose, benefits and form of
     global development goals.

3   *Aid focus too narrow:* Assisting developing countries through
     development cooperation has always been an important means
     of helping to ensure progress towards the achievement of the
     MDGs. It will continue to be important for a number of poor and
     fragile countries, indeed crucial in many cases; the debate on aid
     effectiveness remains topical for this reason. However, the focus
     of development cooperation in the past has helped to exclude
     other areas. The image of the developing country dependent on
     development aid, for example, is becoming increasingly inaccurate.
     If the post-2015 approach is to be global, it should be made clear
     that development cooperation can be only part of the answer. Even
     poor developing countries finance much of their development
     effort themselves from the taxes they raise and so on. Far more
     attention should also be paid to the global framework and the
     world economic order in the post-2015 debates. How, for example,
     can the international financial markets be so organised that they
     are as conducive to development as possible and do not cause
     serious damage should they fail? This is not least in the OECD
     countries' own interests. What are needed in this context are
     innovative approaches, and they could be promoted particularly at
     EU level. A major European contribution might consist in the EU
     seeking to make international regimes in various areas of policy (on
     international capital flows, for instance) development-friendly.

DOI: 10.1057/9781137397881.0007

Notes

1   See, for example, the glossary in OECD / DAC (2012a, 289 ff.).

2   For the development cooperation data in this chapter see,
    OECD / DAC (2012a) and http://www.oecd.org/dac/stats/
    aidtopoorcountriesslipsfurtherasgovernmentstightenbudgets.htm (accessed
    14 May 2013)

3   Data obtained from:
    http://www.oecd.org/dac/aidstatistics/statisticsonresourceflows
    todevelopingcountries.htm (accessed 17 January 2013)

4   Data obtained from:
    http://www.oecd.org/dac/aidstatistics/statisticsonresourceflows
    todevelopingcountries.htm (accessed 17 January 2013)

5   See the definition in OECD / DAC (2012a, 188). 57 per cent of bilateral aid in
    2010 is classified by the DAC as "programmable".

6   See, Klingebiel (2010) for the overview and OECD / DAC (2011b; 2012a) for
    the figures.

7   This section is based, with some amendments, on Janus / Klingebiel (2012).

DOI: 10.1057/9781137397881.0007

2
Development Cooperation Actors: The New Variety of Donors

Abstract: *Various donors engage in development cooperation. The group of traditional donors (Germany, France, the USA, etc.) who together form the OECD's Development Assistance Committee is being complemented by a growing number of "emerging donors" from among the economically dynamic states (China, Brazil, etc.). A distinction is also made in the debate on development policy between bilateral and multilateral development cooperation. This is an indication that certain features of this cooperation may differ according to whether the donor is a single country (bilateral) or an international institution (multilateral).*

Klingebiel, Stephan. *Development Cooperation: Challenges of the New Aid Architecture*. Basingstoke: Palgrave Macmillan, 2014. DOI: 10.1057/9781137397881.0008.

DOI: 10.1057/9781137397881.0008

2.1   "Old donors" – "new donors"

Development cooperation is offered by various donors. Generally speaking, three groups can be distinguished from the models they have adopted (Zimmermann / Smith 2011, 724 ff.):

1   The traditional donors have joined to form the OECD's Development Assistance Committee (DAC). The DAC has 24 members (23 states, including Germany, France the United Kingdom, Japan and the USA, and the Commission of the European Union); the World Bank, the International Monetary Fund (IMF) and the United Nations Development Programme (UNDP) act as observers. The DAC continues to be regarded as the committee of the "classical donor countries" (with the exception of South Korea, which did not become a member until 2010), who provide 70 to 90 per cent of global development cooperation funds. The committee is also an important forum for the recording of development cooperation contributions (statistics and so on) and standards (that is, agreements on definitions, standards and so on). It has defined criteria for "effective aid" and so attempted to reduce the instrumentalisation of development cooperation for other policies (foreign trade interests, security and foreign policy objectives and so on).

2   The group of Arab donors has been engaged in development cooperation since the 1970s; they are not therefore "new donors" in the narrow sense of the term. The group includes Kuwait, Saudi Arabia and the United Arab Emirates, which account for some 90 per cent of Arab development aid (Walz / Ramachandran 2011, 11). At times, Arab donors have made very large amounts of development aid available by comparison with their economic strength (up to 1.5 per cent of GNP). Traditionally, other Arab states have been the main beneficiaries of this aid, although sub-Saharan Africa has been receiving growing support from Arab donors.

3   The third group comprises the "emerging donors", among them China, India, Brazil, Chile, Venezuela, Mexico and South Africa. Their cooperation with developing countries is commonly known as "South-South cooperation", reflecting a horizontal cooperative relationship (rather than the traditional vertical North-South version). Another important distinction from traditional donors is

DOI: 10.1057/9781137397881.0008

a different understanding of development (Brautigam 2009), which is deliberately restrained in political matters (the principle of non-interference). Emerging donors usually stress the mutual benefits of cooperation. Greater emphasis is placed on economic self-interest, and a link to commercial instruments is often an explicit goal (whereas DAC donors strive to avoid mixing development and foreign trade interests). Emerging donors often prefer to cooperate on infrastructure projects (transport infrastructure, energy projects, such public buildings as foreign ministries and so on); resource-rich countries such as Angola, Nigeria and Sudan also play a major role as cooperation partners.

Besides governmental aid donors, there are many non-governmental or private donors. Numerous international non-governmental organisations are engaged in development cooperation and humanitarian assistance. They finance their activities from public contributions and private donations or from members' contributions. Oxfam, CARE and German Agro Action (Deutsche Welthungerhilfe) are examples of large international NGOs.

Since the 1990s more and more private foundations (philanthropic donors), which finance their work from an endowment fund, have been emerging in development cooperation. Their activities have meanwhile assumed significant proportions, equivalent to some 6 to 8 per cent of the DAC donors' contributions. With expenditure of US\$ 2.3 billion, the Bill and Melinda Gates Foundation (BMGF), currently the largest, easily outstrips some smaller donor countries such as Finland and Portugal (Lundsgaarde 2010 and 2013).

BOX 2.1   *German development cooperation: significance, institutions and instruments*

Germany is among the world's leading bilateral donors. In 2012, with development aid amounting to US\$ 13.1 billion, it took third place to the USA and the UK among the DAC donor countries. With its development aid accounting for 0.38 per cent of its national economic strength, Germany does better than the DAC average (0.29 per cent), but less well than the EU average.[1] It provides almost two-thirds of its resources for partner countries in bilateral form. Over a third of its contributions of development aid flows through

DOI: 10.1057/9781137397881.0008

the institutions of the European Union and such multilateral bodies as the World Bank Group and the UN Funds and Programmes (Klingebiel 2012a).

Within the German government, development cooperation is better placed than in various other donor countries in that it has its own ministry (Nuscheler 2006). The Federal Ministry for Economic Cooperation and Development (BMZ), which was set up in 1961, is represented in the Cabinet and is therefore, in principle, in a good position to introduce development issues into debates on German domestic and foreign policy. The BMZ's actual strength depends on a wide range of factors, such as the interests of other ministries (including the Foreign Office and Defence Ministry) and pressure groups. The continued existence of a separate government department for development has been repeatedly questioned in the German political debate. In the German parliament, the Bundestag, a select committee (Committee for Economic Cooperation and Development – AwZ), the BMZ's parliamentary counterpart, considers development issues.

Until recently, German development cooperation had a highly differentiated implementation system, usually considered at international level to be unmanageable and fragmented. A substantial proportion of the BMZ's political management capacities was focused on the internal coordination of the German system (OECD / DAC 2010a). The German implementation system was characterised by an institution in the area of financial cooperation, the KfW Development Bank,[2] and numerous technical cooperation institutions, which, apart from the former GTZ (German Society for Technical Cooperation), specialised, among other things, in the assignment of development aid volunteers and the organisation of training courses for technical experts from developing countries. As a result of the two-phase merging of the technical cooperation organisations, there has been only one such institution since 2011: the GIZ (German Society for International Cooperation). The KfW Development Bank continues to engage in financial cooperation on behalf of the BMZ. The technical cooperation reforms are intended to overcome the former dominance of development implementing organisations over the BMZ and the fragmented implementation in partner countries. At the same time, the previously limited decentralisation of German development cooperation in partner

DOI: 10.1057/9781137397881.0008

countries has been increased under the coalition government's 2009 agreement through a rise in the number of development experts at German embassies.

Like other bilateral donors, Germany has endeavoured to increase the effectiveness of development cooperation by improving its focus. In the future, German development cooperation will be concentrated on an even smaller number of partner countries (57) and focal areas (11). No more than three focal areas are to be supported in any partner country (BMZ 2011).

In the aid allocation process the BMZ applies the following criteria to the selection of partner countries (BMZ 2011):

- ▸ How poor is the country?
- ▸ Can we protect such public goods as climate, world health and peace through cooperation?
- ▸ Does the government pursue a development-friendly policy, and does it intend to advance reforms?
- ▸ What value does Germany add compared to other donors?
- ▸ Has Germany had sustained historical and political relations with the country?
- ▸ Despite various efforts to align German development cooperation more strategically, the 2010 DAC peer review (OECD / DAC 2010a), for example, calls for further conceptual clarification in certain areas (such as the distribution of bi- and multilateral development aid). It also criticises the inadequacy of the steps taken to increase aid effectiveness, referring to the untying of technical cooperation, which is prevented by direct allocation.

2.2   Bi- and multilateral development cooperation

In practice, it is often impossible to make an unequivocal distinction between bi- and multilateral development cooperation, there being various intermediate and special forms. In particular, the development cooperation in which the EU institutions engage differs from multilateral development cooperation.

In recent years questions about the multilateral system of development cooperation have again been under discussion. Two partly overlapping

DOI: 10.1057/9781137397881.0008

debates can be cited in this context. First, the interest of donor countries in new analyses and assessments of the work of individual multilateral institutions has grown. As roughly half of all the members of the OECD's Development Assistance Committee regularly review the balance between bi- and multilateral development cooperation,[3] such investigations influence donors' decision-making processes.

Second, the development cooperation system is characterised by a fairly long-term trend towards the proliferation of actors (Zimmermann / Smith 2011; Severino / Ray 2009) of different types, such as private actors (especially foundations) and emerging donors (China, India, Mexico and so on), and of multilateral financing mechanisms. The growing number of actors is partly to blame for the development cooperation system being perceived as fragmented and disadvantageous, giving rise, among other things, to losses of efficiency due to high transaction costs. Of all the low-income countries, 80 per cent experienced an increase in the number of donors from 2004 to 2009, in some cases by more than 50 per cent (OECD / DAC 2012b, 122). Some experts (for example, Reisen 2009) see the number of multilateral actors as one of the main causes of fragmentation. Other analyses, however, detect the opposite trend: the concentration of multilateral development cooperation being, on the whole, greater and the multilateral system therefore less to blame for fragmentation than bilateral donors.

Differences and intermediate forms

The difference between bi- and multilateral development cooperation is one of the fundamental distinctions in the provision of development aid. It is an indication that certain features of development cooperation depend on whether the donor is an individual state (bilateral development cooperation) or an international institution (multilateral development cooperation).

The multilateral development cooperation category is based on the assumption that the various donor contributions are pooled and so become part of the aid provided by the international institution concerned.[4] In practice, however, it is not always possible to make such an unequivocal distinction between bi- and multilateral development cooperation, there being various intermediate and special forms, the development cooperation in which the European Union engages and international agreements which lead to sectoral or regional quota arrangements even for bilateral development cooperation (Klingebiel 2012a).

DOI: 10.1057/9781137397881.0008

In terms of core contributions to multilateral institutions (including the EU), the OECD's DAC donors provide almost 30 per cent of their development assistance in multilateral form (2011: 27 per cent or US$ 37.6 billion); the proportion has sometimes been higher in the past (2001: 33 per cent).[5] The DAC member countries vary widely in the amount of multilateral assistance they provide. The world's largest donor of development assistance, the USA, makes by far the smallest share available to multilateral bodies (11.5 per cent in 2011), while Italy is the largest (56.7 per cent); at 34.4 per cent, Germany ranks in the "upper middle" (OECD / DAC 2013b).

Recent years have seen a sharp increase in funds flowing through multilateral channels, but earmarked for specific sectors or countries. In some cases, donors have very specific – even minor – projects financed in this way. Such funds are not therefore "genuine" multilateral resources, available to the international institutions as core contributions ("bilateralisation of multilateral development cooperation"), but are spent via multilateral mechanisms. This "multi-bi financing" currently accounts for 12 per cent (US$ 16.5 billion in 2011) of total development financing and is rising fast (OECD / DAC 2013b). Some donors, such as Australia, Canada and the USA, make more funds available in this way than in the form of core contributions. The disadvantages of multi-bi development financing are considerable and outweigh any advantages (piloting certain approaches and so on), this being especially true where non-core contributions by a single donor are concerned (a single trust fund), as opposed to non-core financing by a number of donors (multi-donor trust funds). As non-core contributions increase transaction costs and undermine the governance structures of multilateral institutions, they may help to "dilute" their mandates, since incentives are given to take on all manner of tasks (Mahn 2012; OECD / DAC 2012b, 47–49).

The "emerging donors" vary in their conduct in multilateral development cooperation. The EU Member States that do not belong to the DAC do not, as a rule, have any implementing structures of their own and make relatively large volumes of development aid available through the EU. Russia and Brazil use regional mechanisms in particular, while China and India prefer bilateral approaches (OECD 2011a, 34; UNDESA 2010).

Multilateral development cooperation actors

Multilateral development cooperation actors vary in terms of their significance, tasks and regional or sectoral alignment. As regards the

DOI: 10.1057/9781137397881.0008

volumes of aid available, the development assistance provided by the EU institutions and by the development banks (International Development Association – IDA) and regional banks (for example, the African Development Bank) dominates. Some actors operate globally, while others concentrate on a given region. The Global Fund to Fight AIDS, Tuberculosis and Malaria, a "vertical" fund, is among the most important multilateral actors. At multilateral level there is also, in important sectors at least, a sharing of tasks between development financing (development banks) and technical cooperation (UN Funds and Programmes).

Even though, at some 210 organisations, funds and trust funds,[6] the number of multilateral development cooperation actors is high, a concentration on five main actors or groups of actors is discernible. These actors account for 81 per cent (the average from 2006 to 2010) of all resources spent by the DAC members on multilateral development cooperation (OECD / DAC 2013a, 12):

▸ The European Development Fund (EDF) and the EU's development cooperation budget (36 per cent).
▸ The IDA, which forms part of the World Bank Group (22 per cent).
▸ The UN Funds and Programmes (9 per cent).
▸ The Asian and African Development Banks (3 and 5 per cent, respectively).
▸ The Global Fund to Fight AIDS, Tuberculosis and Malaria (7 per cent).
▸ The other multilateral bodies accounted for only 19 per cent of total multilateral development cooperation.

2.2.1   The specific role of the EU

The development cooperation in which the EU institutions engage, which is financed from the European Development Fund and, to a lesser extent, from the European budget, is equivalent to about 18 per cent of all the development assistance provided by the EU Member States that belong to the DAC, making the European Commission the largest donor in the EU (Klingebiel 2012a). The development assistance provided by the EU institutions in 2010 amounted to US\$ 13 billion; the EU Member States represented on the DAC together account for more than half (55 per cent in 2010) of the DAC members' total global development assistance (OECD 2011b, 140, 154–155).

DOI: 10.1057/9781137397881.0008

Being a supranational donor, the EU is a special case, qualifying for the "multilateral development cooperation" category to only a very limited extent.[7] It is the only member of the DAC that performs a triple function: (i) it itself makes development assistance available to developing countries, (ii) it acts as a donor to multilateral institutions and passes the resources concerned on to them, and (iii) it acts as a catalyst between its Member States and the Commission for coordinated approaches to multilateral institutions and partner countries. Generally speaking, the EU's development cooperation should not be subsumed as part of multilateral development cooperation, but seen as "collective bilateralism" (Klingebiel 1993). Such a categorisation would possibly be relevant in the case of donor countries that have put upper limits on contributions of development assistance to multilateral bodies (OECD / DAC 2012b, 31).

"Complementarity" in development cooperation is an issue for the EU in several respects (Furness 2012a; Grimm 2010). Of prime concern is complementarity between the Union and its Member States. The Maastricht Treaty provided for the policy of the EU institutions to complement the policy of the Member States. The Lisbon Treaty further increased the EU's importance as a separate donor. The EU's policy and that of its Member States are now to complement each other ("shared parallel competences"). Another important and increasingly debated dimension is the complementarity of the various Members States' development cooperation.

The effectiveness of the joint development cooperation of the EU institutions has been significantly improved by a number of reforms since the late 1990s (Grimm 2010). The EU and its Member States face further major challenges in coordinating European development cooperation. This is the aim of the 2007 code of conduct on the division of labour and the initiatives launched with a view to introducing joint programming (Furness 2012a).

2.2.2 Multilateral development cooperation: strengths and weaknesses

Individual donor countries see bilateral cooperation as having various advantages. The donor is able to determine the alignment of the aid far more directly, as regards subject areas and the choice of countries, for example. This makes it more visible both at home (to its parliament, the public and so on) and to the partner country. Similarly, any interests the donor has can be pursued far more directly with bilateral development cooperation through, say, forms of direct or indirect preferential treatment of enterprises in its own country or the use of development cooperation for the sanctioning of partner countries under the donor's foreign policy; direct self-interest usually reduces the benefits of development cooperation that are actually being sought. Frequently, bilateral donors also claim that they are able to act more quickly, flexibly and unbureaucratically than multilateral actors (Klingebiel 2012a). Some donors, among them Switzerland and Germany, have put upper limits on the proportion of multilateral development cooperation as a way of promoting bilateral cooperation (OECD / DAC 2012b, 31–32).

Multilateral development cooperation has other real or supposed advantages and disadvantages. In some respects, partner governments have better means of participating in decision-making processes relating to multilateral cooperation, because they are themselves represented in the supervisory bodies (UN Funds and Programmes, for instance). This increases the legitimacy of development cooperation in partner countries (Fues and Klingebiel 2007). As individual donor countries' own interests can be projected far less clearly, multilateral development cooperation is considered to be less "politicised" and interest-led. Various studies (Keohane et al. 2009) indicate that multilateral institutions and development cooperation may also help to support democratisation processes in countries assisted by reinforcing the rights of minorities, for instance.

The pooling of resources also enables larger tasks that would overstretch individual bilateral donors to be taken on, thus reducing the risk of a piecemeal approach ("projectitis"). In addition, larger risks (in fragile countries, for example) can be taken better communally than bilaterally, and the risk of "aid orphans" can be reduced, since multilateral mechanisms achieve a more even spread of development assistance among countries (OECD / DAC 2012b, 20). Multilateral actors also differ from bilateral actors in some of the tasks they perform. Some UN agencies, for example, have important international standard-setting functions that cannot be performed by bilateral donors (Fues and Klingebiel 2007). Where the EU institutions are concerned, one of the core arguments is that they not only constitute a further European donor, but increasingly perform a coordinating function for the European development cooperation system (Orbie 2012).

Besides the aspects described above, some of which were already under discussion in the 1960s and 1970s, others are growing in importance:

1   *Aid effectiveness and the partner countries' perspective:* Whether bi- or multilateral development cooperation has certain advantages

DOI: 10.1057/9781137397881.0008

or disadvantages should be considered and assessed primarily from the partner's point of view and so in terms of "effectiveness" (Klingebiel 2012a). If a fragmented development cooperation system is, generally speaking, disadvantageous for the partner (high transaction costs, limited transparency, high overheads for maintaining the system and so on), the question is not primarily "bi- and/or multilateral development cooperation" (as it has often been in the past), but more generally whether the donor's supply structure is appropriate. Focusing on "bilateral" or "multilateral" is therefore of only limited help: other aspects (such as aid modalities, opportunities for using national systems and so on) play a major role.

Multilateral development cooperation, or further multilateralisation, can therefore be interpreted as a contribution to the implementation of the aid effectiveness agenda (Manning 2012, 10). The provision of development aid through multilateral bodies leads to efficiency gains (procedures are rationalised, resources pooled and so on); research findings also indicate by and large that multilateral mechanisms make for the effective use of resources.

2   *"New visibility":* Given the new approaches adopted at country level (greater importance attached to multi-donor sectoral dialogues and so on) and the more recent development cooperation approaches to the financing of partners' programmes (pool arrangements, budget support and so on), the question is whether bilateral development cooperation in its present, changed form is more visible, as it is assumed to be. In their assessment of development aid contributions, partner governments and donors represented in partner countries focus far more closely on the effects on development and integration into the partner country's domestic processes (Vollmer 2012), attaching less importance to attributability to a certain donor. The individual project that can be attributed to a specific donor therefore recedes into the background or is even deemed to be disadvantageous for development (distortion of accountability structures). In some cases, a high level of visibility in partner countries is more likely to be achieved through budget support and other contributions to programme financing than through classical, demonstrable bilateral projects. Participation in processes of on-the-spot dialogue is of growing importance for visibility. All in all, then, the classical argument for

DOI: 10.1057/9781137397881.0008

bilateral development cooperation – greater visibility in the partner country – is waning in importance.

3 *Country- and sector-related division of labour:* Against the background of the effectiveness debates, aspects of the division of labour among donors is very important. The sought-after country concentration of bilateral donors is resulting, among other things, in a decline in the number of bilateral donors and in the volume of development assistance in various partner countries (disproportionately "difficult countries"), whereas the large multilateral actors at least are deliberately meant to continue maintaining a broad representative network (multilateral development cooperation as "donor of last resort"). The DFID, for instance, now cooperates with only 28 countries (DFID 2012, 8), while the EU is operating in about 150 (Parliament UK 2012).

4 *Global public goods:* The context in which development cooperation occurs is changing rapidly. Development challenges in the past were viewed particularly at the level of the individual country. Given the cross-border dimension of many aspects (security, impact of climate change, migration, food security and so on), considering them from that angle is no longer appropriate. Development tasks are increasingly considered in connection with the provision of public goods (Kaul et al. 2003; Kaul 2013).   When it comes to participating in the provision of global and regional public goods, multilateral actors have certain advantages. They are more likely to deal with difficulties arising from patterns of collective action better than a variety of individual countries, each with its own approach.

5 *Norms and standards:* The Millennium Development Goals and the aid effectiveness agenda, for example, have confirmed that international norms and standards for global, regional and national policies (of partner countries, donors and so on) can be set only by multilateral actors. Their universal legitimacy means that multilateral organisations alone are capable of this.

2.2.3   Effectiveness of multilateral development cooperation

Two methods in particular can be used to assess multilateral development cooperation: first, targeted performance analyses of the multilateral development cooperation system or of individual multilateral

DOI: 10.1057/9781137397881.0008

institutions and, second, indicators introduced in the past by the OECD and pointers to the viability of multilateral development cooperation.

In the past five to ten years or so, greater efforts have been made to arrive at a more systematic assessment of donors' efficiency – with specific reference, in some respects, to the multilateral institutions. The most important analyses include the following:

▶ The evaluation of the Paris Declaration, the aim being to review the indicators of aid effectiveness. The most comprehensive study by Wood et al. (2011) does not, however, cover the EU's and IDA's development assistance.

▶ The network supported by 16 donors since 2002 for the joint assessment of multilateral aid effectiveness (Multilateral Organisation Performance Assessment Network – MOPAN[8]) by donors. Each year MOPAN carries out four to six joint analyses (OECD /DAC 2013a).

▶ The Quality of Official Development Assistance Assessment (QuODA) (Birdsall und Kharas 2010), which covers a total of 31 bi- and multilateral donors.

▶ Donor studies and research on the multilateral system, such as the Multilateral Aid Review undertaken by DFID in 2011; similar research has been conducted by Australia, the Netherlands and Sweden (OECD / DAC 2013a, 22; OECD / DAC 2013b). Unlike MOPAN, the analyses undertaken by individual donors differ, since the various donor preferences have considerable influence on the research profile (the donor's priorities, which may not form part of the institution's profile).

▶ Reports on individual actors (for example, Bigsten et al. 2011 on the EU).

Despite the available studies, no more than limited generalisations can be made about the quality of bilateral and multilateral development cooperation. This is due to the wide variety of donor groups (both bi- and multilateral) and the widely differing study methods and approaches they adopt.

Nonetheless, most research findings indicate that multilateral development cooperation is, on the whole, satisfactory. The QuODA, for example, shows that, on average, multilateral development cooperation does better than its bilateral counterpart in three of the four quality dimensions covered (Birdsall and Kharas 2010, 24–25). Other studies tend to endorse these assessments (for example, Picciotto 2011).

DOI: 10.1057/9781137397881.0008

How and how far studies on the efficiency of multilateral development cooperation actually influence donors' allocation decisions cannot yet be assessed satisfactorily. Surveys of DAC donors suggest that analyses of their own performance are among the important foundations for allocation decisions.[9]

The perception of EU citizens is that the performance of multilateral organisations is rather good compared to bilateral programmes. Accordingly, the public in 26 of 27 countries rate the quality of large international organisations higher than that of bilateral approaches (OECD / DAC 2012b, 30). As regards the USA, research findings (Milner / Tingley 2012) show that, despite awareness of the effectiveness of multilateral development cooperation, public support for it is limited. With the aid of the principal-agent model, this is ascribed to the basic conflict of objectives between the efficient and effective use of resources (in favour of the World Bank as agent, for example) and the loss of control experienced by the principal (in this case, the USA). In other words, despite possible assumptions concerning the power of the multilateral system, the lack of opportunities for exercising control may result in a multilateral approach receiving no more than limited support.

Performance indicators

In the past, a wide range of (predominantly) input indicators were applied to assess donors and used in research. They include total Official Development Assistance (ODA), regional, income-related and sectoral distribution indicators, distribution to instruments and allocation patterns (proportion of humanitarian assistance, tied aid, etc.).

Additional, more recent OECD data cover the following quantitative and qualitative aspects:

1   Country Programmable Aid (CPA) takes account of the criticism that partner countries have little control over many of the contributions shown as ODA. Such contributions as "student fees" in donor countries for nationals of developing countries and so on cannot be "programmed" by the recipient countries, or to only a limited extent. CPA is a subcategory of ODA that does not include some of the donors' expenditure attributable to ODA (such as administrative costs) and so provides what the partner country sees as a better way of enjoying the benefits of development cooperation (OECD / DAC 2013c). Average CPA figures for

DOI: 10.1057/9781137397881.0008

multilateral institutions and the EU institutions are far higher than those relating to the bilateral development cooperation in which the DAC donors engage. In 2010 the CPA share was 74.0 per cent for all multilateral bodies (excluding the EU), 72.5 per cent for the EU institutions and 55.1 per cent for the DAC donors' bilateral development cooperation.[10]

2   In past years the OECD has presented quantitative analyses covering the "significance" of aid relations, the aid concentration ratio[11] and the fragmentation ratio[12] (see, OECD / DAC 2011c and 2012c). For various reasons, assessing the efficiency of donors from these data is difficult.[13] The available data indicate, however, that bilateral development cooperation causes relatively more fragmentation phenomena than multilateral development cooperation. The multilateral donors' aid concentration ratio[14] is consequently 65 per cent (including the EU; excluding the EU, 62 per cent); in the case of the DAC countries' bilateral development cooperation, on the other hand, it is 54 per cent (OECD / DAC 2013a, 22).

2.2.4   Bi- or multilateral?

By and large, the multilateral development cooperation system was implicitly viewed from two perspectives in the past: one was heavily influenced by the premise that a viable "patchwork approach" could be taken to global challenges. Even the many individual examples of an incoherent multilateral system do not necessarily mean that, given the wide range of different global, regional and national challenges, no synergistic potential is generated by the various multilateral actors. Rather, the wide range of tasks and problems calls for different actors.

The second perspective proceeds from the assumption that the multilateral system is characterised by losses of impact and fragmentation. The system consequently features a wide variety of actors, often performing overlapping tasks and often having only a limited resource endowment. This, it is argued, results in losses of efficiency and effectiveness (transaction costs and so on) for partner countries when aid is provided.

A proliferation of actors is indeed a feature of the whole development aid system. The multilateral aid mechanisms form part of the system and help to bring about losses of effectiveness and efficiency, even if bilateral donors are more to blame. It is therefore wise not to consider multilateral institutions in isolation, but with the institutions of all donor actors included.

A number of studies in recent years have contributed to a better understanding of the multilateral aid system and its actors. These analyses have made it clear that, on average, multilateral aid is to be rated positively. They do not support the proposition that the quality of multilateral aid is unsatisfactory. On that basis, one question for future research should be: what effect do these studies have on donors' allocation decisions? Do they help to change donor governments' and parliaments' preferences and decisions? Or do other criteria have more influence on allocation decisions?

Past years have revealed a trend towards the use of the multilateral system for specific donor interests. This is evident from the change in financing behaviour, in which individual donors' goals are set and achieved by multilateral institutions through multi-bi development cooperation. Donor countries also strengthen the trend through the performance analyses they commission, which are linked to the individual donor's system of objectives rather than that of the multilateral institution concerned.

The EU's development cooperation differs substantially from the work of multilateral actors. The EU is a political community that acts as an independent entity in multilateral institutions (such as the United Nations). The Member States have far more opportunity to influence the EU approach individually than in multilateral institutions with structurally different governance bodies. This difference between multilateral action and approaches adopted by the EU should be taken into account in development cooperation (in the portrayal of bi- and multilateral development cooperation, for instance).

Notes

1   See, OECD / DAC 2012a and http://www.oecd.org/dac/stats/ aidtopoorcountriesslipsfurtherasgovernmentstightenbudgets.htm (accessed 14 May 2013)

2   The KfW Bankengruppe also includes DEG (Deutsche Investitions-und Entwicklungsgesellschaft), which finances and advises private enterprises investing in developing countries.

3   Of the 23 DAC member countries, 11 claim that they reconsider the balance between bilateral and multilateral development cooperation every three to five years (OECD / DAC 2012b, 30).

DOI: 10.1057/9781137397881.0008

4   See the OECD definition, according to which one of the three criteria that
    an institution engaging in multilateral development cooperation must meet
    is the following: "pools contributions so that they lose their identity and
    become an integral part of its financial assets" (OECD 2011a, 23). The other
    two criteria are: (i) the activities of the institution must be at least partly
    geared to promoting development and (ii) the international institution has
    governments as members or a budget which it manages independently.

5   Unless otherwise stated, the data have been obtained from OECD (2011a).

6   See, http://www.oecd.org/dac/aid-architecture/12_10_02%20Policy%20
    Briefing%20on%20Multilateral%20Aid_draft_final_draft%20%282%29.pdf
    (accessed 14 March 2013)

7   The 2011 DAC Report reads: "Even though it is often presented as a
    multilateral in DAC publications, the EU is an individual donor with its own
    development policy and resources." (OECD 2011b, 155).

8   For further details see: http://www.mopanonline.org/

9   See the responses to a DAC donor survey on multilateral development
    cooperation, which are to be found in OECD / DAC (2012b, 32).

10 Calculated from data obtained from OECD / DAC (2013b).

11 From the donor's viewpoint, the degree of "significant" relations with partner
    countries.

12 From the partner's viewpoint, significant relations with donors.

13 Whether a financially significant or non-significant relationship is
    worthwhile for the partner country also depends on various other factors,
    which may be even more important (such as possibly low transaction costs
    in the case of fairly small financial contributions to closely harmonised
    programmes). As regards the number of partners of multilateral institutions,
    what is very important, for example, is whether the mandate provides for
    comprehensive or regional jurisdiction (for example, the universal compass
    of the UN Funds and Programmes versus that of the regional banks).

14 The development cooperation concentration ratio measures the ratio of
    a donor's "significant" to his "non-significant" development cooperation
    relations.

DOI: 10.1057/9781137397881.0008

3

Partner Countries: Differentiating Partners in Developing Regions

Abstract: *Until the 1990s a relatively simple distinction was made between an industrialised and, on average, prosperous "North" and an, on average, poor "South". Processes leading to some differentiation within the group of developing countries had already been taking place in the previous decades. As early as the 1980s the term "emerging economies" indicated that there was a group of more advanced countries in the "South". At the other end of the spectrum were the "least developed countries". This process of differentiation escalated in the 1990s and 2000s, making the image of a homogeneous "South" increasingly inaccurate. The pace of economic development in a number of important developing countries has also been higher than in the OECD world.*

Klingebiel, Stephan. *Development Cooperation: Challenges of the New Aid Architecture*. Basingstoke: Palgrave Macmillan, 2014. DOI: 10.1057/9781137397881.0009.

In a long-term view, the group of countries recognised as recipients of aid by the OECD/DAC donor group has undergone sweeping changes. From 1970 to 2010, 15 more "recipients" were added to the list, while 35 were removed (OECD / DAC 2011b, 225). On the one hand, the adjustments reflect political changes and assessments, as a result, say, of the collapse of the Soviet Union and the consequent need to include new countries as separate "recipients", or a new political environment due to the removal of the apartheid system in South Africa, for example. On the other hand, they reflect the economic progress made by developing countries, the majority of those dropped from the list being countries that had been able to achieve substantial revenue growth (for example, Qatar and Singapore).

The growing convergence of features of development in the industrialised world (OECD countries) and the formerly non-industrialised countries (see, Spence 2011) is underlined by South Korea's membership of the OECD's Development Assistance Committee since 2010. This marks the continuation of a structural change that includes not only the differentiation of the "South" but also a rearrangement of groups and coalitions of countries. Not only the profiles of individual countries are changing, but also global processes of debate and negotiation (evident, for example, from the formation of the Group of 20 – G20) and global constellations and perceptions of actors (Rise of the Global South) (see, Chaturvedi / Fues / Sidiropoulos 2012).

Classifications of countries continue to be based on income groups; this is also true of the OECD/DAC list of recipients and comparable country categories. Such a classification system is vital for development cooperation, since it groups potential recipients by need or lack of resources (that is, countries below an income threshold). This approach is coming under pressure for two reasons:

▸ First, the global welfare situation is undergoing a fundamental structural change to the benefit of the "South". Development cooperation is based on an approach to redistribution which presupposes that the group of donors holds a substantial proportion of the world's economic power and is prepared to provide some of it for developing countries in the form of aid. Conversely, the model assumes that developing countries have a serious shortage of resources and therefore need aid. The aid system therefore features a North-South dichotomy. However, this view gives an increasingly distorted picture of the real situation.

DOI: 10.1057/9781137397881.0009

Globally, a significant shift in the global welfare situation occurred in the 2000s; this structural change is likely to persist (see, Spence 2011; OECD 2010). Aside from the OECD economies, a number of countries in the "East" and "South" have evolved as centres of gravity; such developing countries as China and Brazil have risen to become relevant global economic actors. The global economic changes are accompanied by a new global constellation of forces in which developing countries will gradually be able to make and assert claims to political as well as economic power.

▸ Second, existing country classifications do not adequately reflect the processes of differentiation. In view of the economic dynamism of some developing countries, the distinction between them and OECD countries and other more advanced countries is becoming increasingly invalid or blurred. Making a distinction between "developed countries" and "developing countries" is no longer a suitable means of classification (Harris / Moore / Schmitz 2009; Koch 2012). The question for policy is how, given the variety of types of development (from dynamically growing countries to stagnating or barely dynamic countries), country categories should be adjusted and developed further. While the commonly used income groups are largely unsuitable, new country typologies, such as the "four-speed" model or the "multispeed world" approach adopted by the OECD Development Centre (OECD 2010), cannot yet be described as mature, since they are no more than partially capable of coping with methodological and substantive problems (growth orientation and so on).

Although the number of poor or stagnant countries is falling, a core group meeting the aid allocation criterion "countries in need" will persist for the foreseeable future. The statistical designation Least Developed Country (LDC) does not adequately reflect the progress such countries have made in their development.[1] Some significant changes occurred in the group of LDCs and poor developing countries (Low-Income Countries – LICs) in the 2000s; this is especially true of the sub-Saharan African region, which is particularly important for the group of LDCs and LICs (Radelet 2010).

Owing to the major structural changes, then, the number of countries that can be given preferential treatment as aid recipients is falling. The grading of countries is resulting, on average, in a decline in the importance

DOI: 10.1057/9781137397881.0009

of aid to recipients (as a proportion of a country's economic strength, for instance) and in a growing number of developing countries no longer seeing themselves as aid recipients. In addition, commitments by donors and international aid standards (target figures for poor countries and so on) at least tend to argue against continued support for more advanced countries.

3.1   The four-speed world

Until the 1990s what was a comparatively simple distinction from a development perspective was made between an industrialised and, on average, wealthy "North" and an, on average, poor "South". Even in the previous decades processes leading to distinctions being made within the group of developing countries had been taking place. The term "emerging economies" was already an indication in the 1980s that there was a group of more advanced countries in the "South" (see, Stamm 2004). At the other end of the spectrum were the "least developed countries", where a large proportion of the population lived in absolute poverty.

As this process of differentiation continued at a faster pace in the 1990s and 2000s (Koch 2012), the image of a homogeneous "South" became increasingly inaccurate. The pace of economic development in a number of important developing countries was also more rapid than in the OECD world. In the 2000s China and India achieved growth rates averaging three to four times higher than the OECD countries. Globally, then, it is appropriate to form country categories that conform only partly to the old North-South divide. A division into the following four groups is recommended (OECD 2010):

1   *Wealthy countries:* Most OECD countries and equally, in the future, former developing countries that are undergoing particularly rapid development.
2   *Dynamic (converging) countries:* A number of rapidly growing Asian and Latin American countries (middle-income countries).
3   *"Formerly poor countries":* Various poor countries (such as Ghana) which have meanwhile graduated to the group of middle-income countries. Although these countries have made some progress, social challenges and inequalities often persist.
4   *Poor and poorest countries:* For the foreseeable future there will continue to be a fairly large group of poor and poorest countries,

DOI: 10.1057/9781137397881.0009

TABLE 3.1 *New growth geography in the "four-speed world" (number of countries)*

	1990s	2000s
Wealthy countries	34	40
Converging countries	12	65
Slowly emerging economies	66	38
Poor countries	55	25
Total	167	168

Source: OECD (2010).

although their number will gradually decline. There are 48 poorest countries, mostly in sub-Saharan Africa (33), only one being in Latin America (Haiti). Progress in the development of many of these countries is being obstructed by violent conflict or serious governance deficiencies.

3.2   The new geography of poverty

Poverty reduction has been the fundamental principle of action taken under development policies since the basic needs and poverty orientation of the 1970s and 1980s. In the 2000s this development policy paradigm was reaffirmed and developed further by the analyses undertaken by the development economists Jeffrey Sachs (2005) and Paul Collier (2008) among others. On the basis of those analyses, development actors endeavoured to achieve a wider focus of development cooperation on poverty or the Millennium Development Goals through allocation decisions to the benefit of poor countries (LDCs or LICs) or of recipients in sub-Saharan Africa; the functional and regional features were seen to overlap in many respects. As analyses were also influenced by the assumption that "poor countries" (which are often characterised by fragility) and "poor population groups" were largely the same, the orientation of development cooperation to poor countries was seen as synonymous with poverty orientation.

More recent analyses in the early 2010s prompt a fresh look at the global poverty problem:

▸ *The global poverty problem will wane in importance in the longer term, but will persist in individual countries and regions*: Viewed in the

DOI: 10.1057/9781137397881.0009

longer term, poverty is decreasing both in absolute terms and as a relative proportion of the population. In 2008, 1.29 billion people were having to manage on less than US$ 1.25 a day, compared to 1.94 billion in 1981. In 2008, 22 per cent of the population of developing countries were living below the threshold, compared to 52 per cent in 1981. The global success in combating poverty has been largely due its reduction in China (see, Chen / Ravallion 2012).

▶ *Poverty is not a phenomenon confined to poor countries, but principally a challenge to the middle-income countries*: The analyses carried out by Sumner (2010 and 2012) revealed that the distribution of poor people between low- and middle-income countries has changed significantly, contradicting the analyses of Collier (2008), for instance (see, Koch 2012). Most poor people live in middle-income rather than poor countries; considerable income disparities are to be found in many of the more dynamic middle-income countries. In 2007–2008, 72 per cent of the poor lived in middle-income countries (MICs), as against a mere 7 per cent 20 years earlier. These changes are largely due to statistical effects and classifications and especially to the graduation of LICs to MIC status. Development policy prescriptions (such as the concentration of aid on poor countries) mean, however, that these changes are of considerable relevance to aid allocation decisions.

▶ *Enlarging the poverty agenda – development paradigms*: Even in the past the debate on development assistance paradigms went beyond a "narrow concept of poverty" or "income poverty"; Nohlen and Nuscheler (1982), for example, introduced a multidimensional system of targets ("magic pentagon"[2]). In development practice, the concept of "human development", the basis of the Human Development Index calculated by UNDP since 1990, became the alternative to the hitherto dominant growth-fixated development model, which was promoted primarily by the World Bank. Not least because of the income growth in many developing countries and the emergence of new middle classes, two conceptual extensions are significant: first, in view of the economic progress made, the question of the ecological sustainability of development models is of vital importance (natural resource consumption, emissions and so on) (see, WBGU 2011). A development paradigm that does not reflect the limits to the natural environment neglects fundamental

DOI: 10.1057/9781137397881.0009

conditions. Second, aspects of internal distribution are continuing to grow in importance. The growth dynamics of the 2000s led to an increase in inequality in many places and assumed substantial explosive force owing to the growing expectations of middle classes that were gaining in strength. Questions of societal cohesion are therefore of crucial importance for development processes (see, OECD 2011b).

3.3   Development and security policy instruments for conflict management in fragile states and in dealings with them

The lack of state structures, poorly functioning or inadequately legitimised governments and the resultant problems pose a major challenge in several developing-country regions. Sometimes, it is a question of particularly difficult cases of failed states, but often of "vulnerable" or "susceptible" systems too. In the latter case, although the state may well be highly effective, it is possibly incapable of holding sway throughout the country, or its representatives do not have sufficient legitimacy.

In the academic debate and in political practice there is no lack of fundamental awareness that weak and failing statehood is highly relevant to the countries and people directly concerned, to the regional environment and, not least, to international policy. Since the 1990s fragile states have become – in a wide variety of areas of international policy – a central issue. Signs of crisis, violent conflict and radically changing systems are evidence of the persistently marked relevance of the issue in various regions of the world, be it in the Arab world since early 2011, in the countries of the Sahel zone, in the Great Lakes region of Central Africa, in the Democratic Republic of Congo or in and around Afghanistan.

The term "fragility" is widely used, but not necessarily quite accurately. In the international debate the OECD's definition finds relatively wide acceptance. It defines a fragile region or a fragile state as being virtually incapable of performing basic governance functions or of entering into a mutual, constructive exchange with society. Fragile states are, moreover, susceptible to such internal and external shocks as economic crises and natural disasters.[3]

Currently, the OECD classifies 47 states as fragile (see, OECD / DAC 2013a, 17). Most of them – 26 in number – form part of the group of

DOI: 10.1057/9781137397881.0009

low-income countries, examples being Burundi, Afghanistan, Haiti and Somalia. However, 21 middle-income states, including Angola, Kosovo, Nigeria, Sri Lanka and South Sudan, are also represented.

In 2007 the political scientist Marina Ottaway made a helpful comparison between "fragile" and "functioning" states (see, Ottaway 2007, 11–20). She argued that the goal of developing a functioning state is extremely hard to achieve because the structure involved is highly complex and that it is equally important to recognise the state as a whole and to take its legitimacy and structures and its efficiency into account. This may preclude hasty, technical approaches to an explanation in which the interlinking of governance challenges in particular is underestimated. The concept of fragility therefore takes account of the complexity of different situations and development deficiencies that may find expression in the poor governance of poorly performing or conflict-affected states.

Consequences of fragility

Fragility is relevant primarily from a humanitarian and poverty-related viewpoint and from a security and stability viewpoint.

Instability and, above all, armed conflicts are two of the main causes of the lack of success in development or any regression that may occur (see, World Bank 2011a). Some 1.5 billion people live in countries and areas characterised by such a situation. No low-income country classified as fragile or affected by violent conflict will be able to achieve the international community's Millennium Development Goals by 2015. Studies also show that conflict-affected countries have a poverty rate that is 21 percentage points higher than those unaffected by conflict. Moreover, fragile states often have an impact on their neighbours, causing reduced growth, for instance. A country like Tanzania, for example, loses about 0.7 per cent of its growth annually for any conflict fought in a neighbouring country.

Also highly relevant are the structurally long-term destabilising effects on the conflict-affected countries themselves and the risks to international security emanating from fragile states. Countries already affected by conflict are at a significantly higher risk of being affected by conflict again. There is an approximately 40 per cent risk that post-war countries will again be overcome by civil war within a decade (see, Hoeffler 2012, 4). Consequently, security strategies, such as that of the USA or the European Union, attach considerable importance to the problems of fragile states. For the international community it is not least the use of

DOI: 10.1057/9781137397881.0009

fragile states as areas to which terrorist groups can withdraw that poses a persistent and, in some cases, growing threat in various regions, including the Sahel zone. The effects of weak and failing states on the countries immediately affected and their people are thus huge, and as they also cross the borders of those states, they influence both the regional context and international security.

Starting-points for development cooperation

A question that is difficult to answer is what can be done to combat the causes and consequences of fragile statehood (World Bank 2011a). This applies not least to the contributions that such external actors as bi- and multilateral donors or international organisations might make. The cases in which the absence of state structures can be remedied from outside in part and within a limited timeframe are, on the whole, rare and, as a general rule, likely to remain exceptions, the financial resources and military capacities being either unavailable or impossible politically to mobilise. And withdrawal from such situations is almost always a far more complicated and lengthy process than initially hoped. At the other end of the spectrum of possible options is the non-engagement of the international community or of its most important governmental and non-governmental actors.

In principle, influence can be brought to bear on weak or failing states from outside with a number of policies, principal among them being foreign, security and development policy.

What can development cooperation achieve? First of all, development cooperation has to do with fragile statehood in almost all its forms and phases. In the long term, it can help to secure stability where systems are relatively well consolidated, assist development-oriented regimes in weak states with the installation of viable structures and create incentives for government action in failing and, in some instances, collapsed states. Frequently, the provision of aid is particularly important in immediate post-war situations as a means of preventing a renewed descent into violent conflict. Development cooperation can be shown to help to increase the benefits of peace dividends in post-war societies (see, Hoeffler 2012).

Reforms of the security sector are often vital if, for example, political monitoring bodies are to be at all able to perform their task of supervising state security actors (military and police) appropriately. In view of the considerable importance of functioning civil and military structures at regional level, such continental or subcontinental institutions as the

DOI: 10.1057/9781137397881.0009

African Union and the Economic Community of West African States (ECOWAS) are often crucial, not least when it comes to legitimising and undertaking military operations from outside, an example being the operation in Mali (in early 2013). Development cooperation can make a significant contribution to the development of appropriate regional mechanisms.

For an understanding of the development perspective of fragile statehood the following substantive links are also important: first, in the late 1990s the debate on the most effective possible use of development cooperation resources led to some concentration on "good performers". In the OECD's Development Assistance Committee and similar fora a question being considered in depth is therefore how countries deemed to be fragile and receiving little development aid compared to their needs should be treated in the future (see, OECD / DAC 2012c). Given the specific needs of fragile states when development aid is used, a group of 19 fragile and conflict-affected countries have joined with development partners and international organisations with a view to placing cooperation with this specific group of countries on a new basis under the heading "A New Deal for Engagement in Fragile States". Part of this newly developed approach is an attempt to improve the management of resources, including development aid, and so to underpin donor confidence in development approaches in fragile states.

Second, a conceptual change has occurred in development cooperation: while one-off, crisis-related measures were developed in the early and mid-1990s and that approach was developed further in the latter half of the decade into a civil crisis prevention concept, the conceptual focus now is on overarching approaches to helping to ensure stability and security. The main aim in this is to achieve more closely networked thinking and action among the security, foreign and development policy actors (see, Klingebiel / Roehder 2008). This does not in any way exclude conflicts of objectives or differing approaches by the actors involved, the question being, for example, "Whose security is the focus of an operation, the local population's or the donor countries'?" or "How is the success of an engagement to be measured?"

Third, the focus of development policy approaches has increasingly shifted to the state and, therefore, to governance issues as seen by fragile states, there being much substantive overlapping with such other topics as democracy promotion, decentralisation, direct crisis prevention and conflict management.

DOI: 10.1057/9781137397881.0009

Integrated policy approaches

Violent conflict may be the expression of acute fragility in a country or region. How it can be confronted with civil and military approaches is among the major questions and challenges facing international policy. For this there are not least the following two reasons:

First, the question is what steps the international community is prepared to take in heightened violent situations which may lead to or entail a humanitarian disaster. Military resources can and must only ever be used as a last resort. Civil approaches to preventing or ending violent conflict are recognised as clearly having priority over military approaches. This is true especially because of the many difficult situations in which military resources cannot make a constructive contribution, and ultimately, only when the specific circumstances of the individual case have been considered can it be determined whether such resources may help to reduce human suffering and to restore stability in the long term. Military approaches are, after all, associated with major uncertainties and risks for all concerned. All relevant international actors proceed very selectively where military intervention is to be considered and where it should be dismissed as an option. In this process, the scale of a local human catastrophe is only one aspect of many to be considered before individual states or the international community as a whole take their decision. For this very reason, the debate on the "responsibility to protect" focuses on this challenge (see, Brock / Deitelhoff 2012).

Second, the benefit of military operations is often unclear (see, Debiel / Goede 2011). More precisely, it is often less an individual, brief military operation – with all the associated complexity and responsibility – that determines success or failure. The question is rather how pacification fits into a wider concept. Can the physical protection of a country or region really be guaranteed by external actors in the long term? What form does the transition to "normal" conditions take? What happens if the stable conditions hoped for simply refuse to come about? The international community often experienced all this in the 1990s and 2000s.

And yet it has been unable to find any really good answers to these questions. It has in fact not replaced government functions at all, or only inadequately, on a number of occasions, and it has been unable to install any permanently viable structures; of this Afghanistan is a particularly impressive example. The main weakness, it has been found, is that the installation of new government structures is extremely complicated. This

DOI: 10.1057/9781137397881.0009

affects the ability of the government apparatus to function and assert itself, which is frequently questioned by non-governmental actors, and also the legitimacy of new regimes, which is not by any means to be achieved automatically or in the short term.

Both topics show how important it is to include the civil and military views. Where a military operation is undertaken and is necessary, it is not enough to create peace structures for the long term. And where civil approaches to preventing or terminating violent conflict are not enough, military steps may need to be taken to avert an acute risk of genocide, for example. These interfaces between the civil and the military are very important at several levels and have attracted increased attention for some fifteen years.

In some cases, as in the US approach, the interfaces are defined from a purely military perspective. How, for example, can such civil measures as reconstruction help to create a favourable environment for a military stabilisation operation and so increase the safety of military personnel? What is all too often overlooked is that, regardless of this, civil action must have an independent role to play. Ultimately, it will be civil approaches in particular that are capable of initiating long-term movement towards political, economic and social stabilisation. Where conditions are persistently fragile, military involvement may continue to be essential, but, here again, an appropriate division of labour is of the utmost importance.

What form might such a division of labour take? How can civil and military actors complement each other appropriately? The relationship between development and security is not a fundamentally new topic (see, Rietjens / Bollen 2008; Klingebiel / Roehder 2008). Much the same can be said of the specific interfaces between different externally oriented policies – development, foreign and security policy in particular. In the past too, the question of the conditions that must prevail as regards stability and peace if development is to be at all possible has at least implicitly played an essential role. In earlier debates, however, this relationship was seen primarily as abstract interdependence. In the debates of the past ten to fifteen years, on the other hand, the combination has been considered far more directly in conceptual and practical, political terms.

The radical change in the concept of security is particularly significant in these debates (see, Daase 2010). The earlier, state-centred concept has given way to new thinking in many areas. Security has been developed fundamentally in the international debate from a concept oriented towards state stability to a protective approach related to the individual human being. Although this does not always have practical implications in political action, they are certainly in evidence in various other spheres. The change from the former Organisation of African Unity (OAU) to the African Union (AU), which has expressly distanced itself from the principle of non-interference, is a clear example of this, even though the implementation of this policy is making no more than slow progress (see, Gänzle / Franke 2010; Klingebiel et al. 2008).

Many of the implications of this change in thinking and of new concepts of development and security are still very difficult to assess. This is true, for example, of the treatment of states that are not sufficiently capable in the long term of gaining what is at best their legitimate monopoly of power. This increasingly gives rise to a confrontation with old patterns of thought (see, Grävingholt / Hofmann / Klingebiel 2007): in what circumstances should or must there be interaction or cooperation with groups which, though having instruments of power, are not legitimised by the state? How to deal with state representatives who, though capable of securing a monopoly of state power, do not have sufficient legitimacy? This will continue to necessitate numerous debates that help to develop further the understanding of the development-security nexus.

Dealing with the tension

On the whole, fragile countries represent one of the main challenges for international policy and not least for development cooperation. Development cooperation has means of promoting governance approaches, helping to install state structures or offering incentives for development-oriented action. Instability and insecurity, poor governance and weak implementation capacities are features of fragile states. They are inconsistent with favourable conditions for development cooperation. On the other hand, effective development policy contributions to solving these problems are particularly relevant. It is therefore essential to seize and increase the opportunities for taking action that development policy provides and to focus the debates not on "how" rather than "whether". Furthermore, the need for coordination and cooperation between civil and military actors in violent conflicts has grown. This interplay too is necessary, though difficult, since the approaches, instruments and even practical objectives often differ.

DOI: 10.1057/9781137397881.0009

3.4   Sub-Saharan Africa: core region for development cooperation?

The conditions facing development cooperation along with other external policies and internal actors in sub-Saharan Africa is changing rapidly and fundamentally. In the past, sub-Saharan Africa was the least dynamic developing region and therefore the most dependent on development cooperation. Changes can be identified in three respects: (1) in the country groups of the region and the change in their view of or need for development financing, (2) with regard to economic preconditions and governance and (3) in the structure of development financing.

The countries of sub-Saharan Africa have undergone processes of change at different speeds and, to some extent, in different directions in the past two decades. Existing country classifications provide no more than the beginnings of suitable categories for the process of differentiation that is taking place. With the help of the IMF classifications, a rough distinction in development financing terms is made here between four groups[4] (see, IMF 2012; Klingebiel 2012b).

Country differentiation

Oil-exporting countries (seven countries with a population of about 214 million people): The oil-exporting countries (over 30 per cent of export revenue coming from oil) of sub-Saharan Africa have resources that enable them to make extensive investments themselves; some other countries that depend heavily on exports of minerals have similar features. The main challenge – facing Equatorial Guinea, for instance – is posed by the management of available resources. The risk of their not being invested in longer-term development processes, but consumed, and of clientelistic structures and inequality being promoted tends to be high. The need for financing through development cooperation and thus dependence on it are limited in this group of countries (examples being Nigeria and Angola, only about half of a percentage point of whose economic strength is dependent on development aid), although some donors pursue economic interests with such aid. The very prospect of future oil revenues – as in Ghana and Uganda – is leading to a decline in the importance and influence of development cooperation.

Middle-income countries (eleven countries with a population of some 105 million people): Characteristic of this group of countries is that foreign direct investment is relatively important for their manufacturing

DOI: 10.1057/9781137397881.0009

sectors. This investment is less vulnerable to international crises, since it is of a long-term nature and tends to be invested in the development of value chains. The countries themselves – among them, Mauritius, South Africa and Botswana – have a considerable interest in providing their own investment in the form of human capital and implementing strategies to promote the private sector. This group of countries is generally interested in longer-term foreign direct investment. The influence of development cooperation is mostly insignificant and declining.

Low-income countries (14 countries with a population of about 342 million people): These countries (such as Ethiopia and Tanzania) are still heavily dependent on development cooperation, which is concentrated on longer-term poverty reduction objectives. Public investment is largely dependent on external support. In certain countries in this group the private sector is developing dynamically, although such development often begins at a low level. Some countries may succeed in joining the middle-income group in the medium term. Financing needs in this group are high in some cases because of limited internal revenue and existing challenges (as in the case of energy and transport infrastructure). In general, development aid is a dominant feature of external financing in this group; this dependence may be gradually reduced by a relatively dynamic private sector and foreign investment.

Fragile countries (twelve countries with a population of some 138 million people): this group is heavily dependent on development assistance. The countries in the group (including Burundi and the Democratic Republic of Congo) are characterised by governance challenges and limited capacities for reform, because political instability and clientelistic structures often dominate. Public investment, financed from domestic revenues and development aid, is at risk of not been implemented effectively. Development aid frequently contributes to stabilisation aimed at counteracting signs of state dissolution. Private investors concentrate their activities not on value chains that might stimulate long-term development, but – if at all – on the exploitation of minerals and other natural resources. The revenue this generates is seldom available for development processes. All in all, development aid and, to some extent, humanitarian assistance are very important for the functioning of these countries and for the provision of a minimum of public services.

For development cooperation the question, especially in countries in which dependence on development aid is limited and continuing to fall, is whether further involvement is still wise in development terms. In the

DOI: 10.1057/9781137397881.0009

debate, views tend to be split between advocates of focusing development cooperation on "poor countries" and advocates of approaches that see worthwhile tasks equally in dynamic and advanced countries (for example, catalytic functions relating to private inflows).

Economic and political trends

Economic trends: Sub-Saharan Africa's economic strength has increased since the 1990s (see, Radelet 2010). Nonetheless, major differences among the countries of sub-Saharan Africa and disparities within individual countries – South Africa, for instance – persist. The question of the quality of growth is similarly important, since structural development processes are not necessarily accompanied by an economic boom. In resource-rich countries (such as the oil-exporters), for example, governance is often inadequate (widespread corruption, insufficient long-term investment and so on). On average, the African economies remain volatile, since many have yet to diversify. Yet in the past ten years or so a group of relatively successful economies has emerged. The International Monetary Fund (IMF 2012) refers to a total of eleven countries in the region with comparatively high growth potential (frontier markets), but there are still significant differences from, say, Asian growth economies. One group – about a third of the countries in the region – is, moreover, hardly integrated into the world economy at all.

Sub-Saharan Africa's macroeconomic situation has largely developed in a positive direction not least because of the better policies pursued by the various countries. In the early 1990s most African countries were *de facto* bankrupt, and indebtedness was growing rapidly. The majority of countries had enormous budget deficits, many of them with two-digit rates of inflation, government intervention, capital flight and black markets. The new situation is therefore identifiable primarily from their foreign debts. Of the 33 African countries that qualified for the debt relief initiative for Heavily Indebted Poor Countries (HIPCs), 29 have meanwhile reached at least the first debt relief step. On average, the sub-Saharan African countries have today to spend less than 5 per cent of their export revenues on debt servicing, compared to the significantly higher figure of almost 16 per cent in 1995 (see, Klingebiel 2012b).

Consequently, Africa's public budgets have more room for manoeuvre today than they had in the past. This enables governments to be more creative (in investment and reform programmes, for instance) and to take more responsibility. With domestic revenue averaging 18 per cent of

GDP (see, Klingebiel 2012b), a substantial proportion of their expenditure is earnt by the sub-Saharan African countries themselves and is available to finance development.

Trends in governance: The quality of governance in the countries of the region plays a principal role for financial inflows in many respects. This is true of private and public inflows alike, where, for example, attractiveness to private investors or canvassing for development aid is concerned.

Generally speaking, the past two decades have seen improvements in political governance (see, Lundsgaarde / Roch 2012). From a global viewpoint, the most significant advances have been made in sub-Saharan Africa and in Europe's transformation countries. This is not to say, however, that there has not also been regression in some countries or years (as revealed, for example, by an annual comparison of Mo Ibrahim Index figures). Many countries of the region have yet to undertake reforms to improve the political environment (with the emphasis on democratisation).

In *economic governance* sub-Saharan Africa lags well behind all other regions of the world. The 2013 international *Doing Business* ranking shows that sub-Saharan Africa occupies, on average, 140th of 185 places, which indicates a serious need for reform (see, World Bank / IFC 2012, 3 f.). Considering the situation over time, however, reveals that it is gradually improving.

Public Financial Management (PFM) is a core dimension of governance. PFM includes not only the administration of public finances, but also budgetary institutions and procedures, that is, the work of parliamentary budget committees, national audit offices and budget planners. The aim of PFM reforms is to achieve more transparent, more effective and more efficient handling of state revenue and expenditure. Suitable analytical instruments make it possible today to assess the efficiency of public financial management. It is becoming apparent that a number of countries (such as Rwanda and Mauritius) have established far more efficient PFM systems than they had in the past. Nonetheless, clientelistic and neo-patrimonial systems continue to dominate in a large number of countries (see, Klingebiel / Mahn 2011).

Change in development financing

International financial flows to sub-Saharan Africa increased sixfold in the past decade (2000–2009) (Klingebiel 2012b). This sharp rise was

DOI: 10.1057/9781137397881.0009

accompanied by a substantial structural change, the proportion of private inflows having grown significantly.

External financial inflows fall into two categories:

1   *Official financial inflows*: In sub-Saharan Africa's case, these include, in particular, Official Development Assistance (ODA), which may take different forms (financial and technical cooperation); in principle, however, other officially provided resources (for export credits, for instance) also fall into this category. Since 2000 the volume of development aid in absolute terms has continued to grow. Sub-Saharan Africa currently receives about US$ 44 billion (2010, net) each year, its share of total ODEC development aid being relatively stable at around 30 per cent (see, OECD/DAC 2011b; 2012a).

The contribution that development aid makes to growth is disputed by researchers; study findings are ambiguous (see, Radelet 2006). Average dependence on development aid in the region (as a share of GDP) has fallen in recent years as economic efficiency has risen.

Official inflows other than development aid (export credits, for example) have hitherto been of limited importance. Besides the OECD countries' contributions, there is growing cooperation between "emerging donors" (including China, India, Brazil and the Gulf States) and sub-Saharan Africa. It is assumed that China's development aid to the region is roughly the same as the volume received from a medium-sized traditional donor (such as the Netherlands), but the difference in its nature (more mixing with other cooperation instruments and so on) makes it difficult to compare with traditional development aid.

2   *Private financial inflows* (see, IMF 2012; AfDB et al. 2012; Klingebiel 2012b): Private financial inflows include foreign direct investment (FDI), portfolio investments and migrants' remittances to their home countries. FDI and portfolio investments amount to more than US$ 52 billion (2010, net) a year (FDI: US$ 32.6 billion; portfolio investment US$ 20 billion) and are thus on roughly the same scale as development aid. In sub-Saharan Africa there is a heavy concentration on just a few countries, some two-thirds of all investments going to South Africa, Nigeria and Angola, with investments in oil and mineral production accounting for

DOI: 10.1057/9781137397881.0009

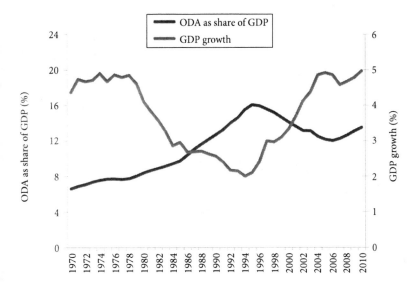

FIGURE 3.1 *ODA as share of GDP and growth rates in sub-Saharan Africa (moving average for 10 years)*

Source: Author's own compilation, World Bank data.

a similarly large share. Officially recorded migrants' remittances to sub-Saharan Africa are rising sharply and amount to US$ 20.8 billion annually (2009).

Two other aspects are relevant to private inflows: first, investment from the African region itself is playing a growing role. South Africa is an important actor in this respect, being active primarily in southern Africa. Second, regional integration has been making gradual progress, examples being the Southern African Development Community (SADC) and the East African Community (EAC). Economic communities are particularly important pull factors for foreign investors who are not active in the oil and minerals sector.

Differentiation in the situation of the sub-Saharan African countries has thus continued to grow in recent years. Some countries have resources of their own that are available for development financing and very important for development processes. External development financing similarly continues to be vital for most countries, and indeed, the group of countries for which private inflows play a major role is growing

DOI: 10.1057/9781137397881.0009

in size. Development aid often performs a crucial function not only, but above all, in the low-income countries and the fragile states. Such low-income countries as Liberia and Rwanda are making growing efforts to free themselves from their traditional dependence on development aid.

Notes

1   Accordingly, there have been only three graduations from the least development cooperation group in the past (UNCTAD 2011).
2   The "magic pentagon" is composed of (i) growth, (ii) labour, (iii) equality/ justice (structural change), (iv) participation, and (v) independence / autonomy.
3   "A fragile region or state has weak capacity to carry out basic governance functions, and lacks the ability to develop mutually constructive relations with society. Fragile states are also more vulnerable to internal or external shocks such as economic crises or natural disasters. More resilient states exhibit the capacity and legitimacy of governing a population and its territory. They can manage and adapt to changing social needs and expectations, shifts in elite and other political agreements, and growing institutional complexity. Fragility and resilience should be seen as shifting points along a spectrum." (OECD / DAC 2012a, 15).
4   Each country is assigned to one group only. A few countries in the region are left out of account.

DOI: 10.1057/9781137397881.0009

4

Approaches: How Development Aid Is Provided

Abstract: *Development cooperation is offered to partners in very different forms. Which of these forms it takes depends on numerous factors. The widely varying situations of partner countries make it necessary for donors to adopt different approaches. An efficient partner country (such as India) has very precise ideas on how development cooperation can complement its own efforts; it also has a wide range of means of managing and using external aid itself. The situation is very different in countries which have weak structures and whose governments may inspire little confidence (clientelistic governments, fragile countries, etc.). It is important to make use of the partner's capacities in development cooperation, not least when they are weak, with a view to strengthening them in the long term.*

Klingebiel, Stephan. *Development Cooperation: Challenges of the New Aid Architecture*. Basingstoke: Palgrave Macmillan, 2014. DOI: 10.1057/9781137397881.0010.

Development cooperation with partners takes very different forms. The manner in which development aid is provided depends on a wide range of factors. The widely differing situations of partner countries make it necessary for donors to adopt different approaches. An efficient partner country, such as India, has very precise ideas on how development aid can complement its own efforts; it also has numerous means of managing and using such external aid. The situation is very different in countries which have no more than weak structures and whose governments may inspire little confidence (clientelistic governments, fragile countries and so on).

A distinction can be made between the following instruments used to provide development aid (see, Rauch 2009; Ihne / Wilhelm 2006; Nuscheler 2006):

1   Technical cooperation (TC) is intended to support partners
    with advice and know-how, thus helping to develop sustainable
    capacities for managing development processes. Hence the frequent
    reference to capacity development.
2   Financial cooperation (FC) is primarily intended to make resources
    available to enable partner countries to undertake the necessary
    investment and expenditure that is important for development
    processes. FC can take the form, for example, of money for the
    construction of schools or resources for the partner's budget to
    enable poverty reduction programmes to be financed.

Criticism is levelled at both instruments. TC is considered virtually unsustainable in many quarters because development organisations may have a serious interest in providing it through their own advisers and so on (see, Rauch 2009; Actionaid 2011). Measures are often not advertised internationally, and partners have limited capacity to manage projects themselves. Developing countries are therefore frequently critical of TC's "supply orientation". FC is criticised when projects are not advertised internationally (because of aid-tying, for instance) or when they clearly do not match partners' priorities. As a fundamental deficiency may consist not in a lack of financial resources, but in the country's poor management, purely financial support may even be conducive to poor governance.

Some donors respect the division between TC and FC (for example, German development cooperation and the UN Funds and Programmes, which provide TC for the most part), while others have abandoned this

DOI: 10.1057/9781137397881.0010

form of instrumental separation (for example, British and Japanese development cooperation).

A further distinction as regards the implementation of development cooperation concerns what are known as aid modalities. It is made particularly between project support and programme financing (see, Mallet/ Sumner 2013; Janus 2012).

1 Development cooperation projects are planned and implemented by a donor to assist the partner. A specific donor project thus serves to achieve a certain objective. Typically, a project of this kind does not form part of the partner country's normal structures (for example, a standard organisational unit of a ministry), but is a construct developed for the purpose of development cooperation. The advantage may lie in the fact that a development cooperation project can be so arranged and implemented that the preconditions for success are comparatively favourable. One advantage may be, for example, that the project presents opportunities for maintaining a very good fleet of vehicles, organising international workshops and possibly avoiding expensive domestic procurement requirements. The project is therefore relatively flexible (which may be important in post-conflict situations, for example), but possibly limited in its impact, since the project is not suitable as a model. At worst, it may even have adverse effects if, for example, it entices efficient administrative staff away from the partner country's administration with high salaries and so weakens the partner.

2 The aim of programme financing is to assist a programme devised by the partner, not to establish a separate donor project (see, Klingebiel / Leiderer / Schmidt 2007; Janus 2012). The donors' contribution consists in jointly supporting the programme (and so avoiding different approaches), making direct use of the partner country's systems and so strengthening them. Budget support is a form of programme financing. The support is provided as a financial contribution, possibly subject to prior conditions. The most important feature is the dialogue between the donors and the partner about implementation. Programme financing therefore calls for smoothly functioning and trustworthy structures on the partner's side. If this condition is not satisfied, savings can at least be achieved, coherence ensured and the burden on the partner's institutions eased through the donors' adoption of a joint approach (pooling of resources).

DOI: 10.1057/9781137397881.0010

BOX 4.1   *Budget support for Rwanda*

Budget support has contributed to Rwanda's development in five respects since the early 2000s (see, Klingebiel 2011b):

1   Budget support makes a useful contribution to the implementation of Rwanda's national development strategy. Without budget support, the country would have significantly less in the way of financial resources available to lay the necessary foundations for improving living conditions and creating economic growth (through transport infrastructure, for example). Even with development aid, the Rwandan budget is very small, amounting to only about EUR 1.2 billion per financial year (at a population of about 10 million), which is comparable to the budget of a medium-sized European municipality. General and sectoral budget support accounts for some 20 to 25 per cent of the national budget; budget aid donors and the Rwandan government are also at pains to see the country step up its efforts to earn more of its own revenue.

2   In Rwanda, as in other partner countries, budget support is the preferred cooperation instrument, the partners' view being that it enables them to react best to their needs and also to achieve the most sustainable results.

3   For Rwanda budget support is an incentive to implement reform policies. An important factor in Rwanda's favour is its marked willingness not only to outline, but actually to implement reform policies. Budget support also permits the emphasis in the budget to be placed on poverty, public financial management to be strengthened and conditions for the private sector to be improved. In some respects, Rwanda has made considerable progress in implementing some reform policies. It has, for example, substantially improved its World Bank *Doing Business* ranking and its public financial management.

4   Budget support is reinforcing Rwanda's governance structures through the use of national (monitoring) systems and procedures. The Rwandan parliament is one of the leading advocates of budget aid, because its role is strengthened through its scrutiny of the budget (including budget support resources). However, it plays no part in most other forms of development cooperation. Much the same is true of the

DOI: 10.1057/9781137397881.0010

Rwandan national audit office: the fact that it reviews how budget support is used upgrades it politically. Similarly, budget support reinforces Rwandan procedures for advertising public contracts.

5   Finally, budget support makes a major contribution in Rwanda to improving donor harmonisation and so the effectiveness and efficiency of development cooperation. It is discussed with all the participating donors and the partner, which enables conflicting recommendations, competition for the "best projects" and so on to be largely avoided.

At the same time, budget support is an instrument on which political views are having a greater impact. Since mid-2012 various donors have been hesitant about making disbursements of budget support to the country or have suspended them. This conduct has been prompted by a report from UN experts identifying interference by Rwandan agencies in the conflict in the eastern Democratic Republic of Congo.

4.1   Results-based development cooperation approaches

In principle, all development cooperation approaches are aimed at achieving "results". The international debate on results-based approaches differs from previous debates in that development cooperation is in practice often geared to inputs and processes. In many cases, the resources are intended for investment (in the construction of schools, for example) or advisory services (for the education sector, for instance), but it is often impossible to show "results" (in the sense of outputs and especially outcomes) as proof of the success of the development cooperation measures. Development cooperation successes are instead recorded with the help of input and process indicators, showing, for example, whether expenditure on a country's education sector is increasing or whether agreed reform documents (such as a sectoral strategy for education) have been approved. Although an approach of this kind says something about how development activities in a partner country can be assessed, the information content is limited for two reasons: first, it is often unclear or not ensured that the results sought have actually been achieved. Are, for example, more children being educated because of the increase in

DOI: 10.1057/9781137397881.0010

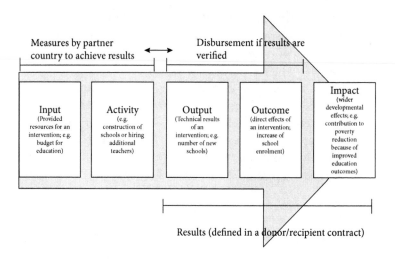

FIGURE 4.1   *RBA effect chain*
Source: Author's own compilation.

expenditure on education and the advisory services provided? What level do school-leavers reach in their education? Second, precisely what part does development aid play in the situation? If results have been achieved, are they causally linked to the development cooperation activity?

Results-based approaches focus on this point and seek to identify quantifiable and measurable results that can be attributed as directly as possible to the effects of the support received through development cooperation. A basic distinction can be made between two debates on results-based approaches (see, Pereira / Villota 2012; Klingebiel 2012c):

1   **Results-based aid** (RBA) approaches are a new form of contractual relationship between the donor and the partner government. The Cash on Delivery concept developed by the Centre for Global Development (CGD) has been a particular subject of debate in recent years (see, Birdsall / Savedoff 2010).

   RBA identifies an accurately defined result. Only when that result has been achieved is a previously specified amount of aid handed over. This contribution should be sufficient an incentive to ensure that the work is actually done. Each agreed step forward is assisted or rewarded *ex post*. Goal achievement is measured and assessed by an independent third party.

DOI: 10.1057/9781137397881.0010

An RBA contract of this kind may provide, for example, that the partner government is to receive a certain amount for every pupil graduating from the school system (measured against generally recognised quality standards). That amount is paid over annually, for example, on the achievement of the target, without any further conditions. This form of development aid seeks not so much to reflect the costs incurred in achieving the target as to act as an appropriate incentive to the partner country to remove obstacles to development consisting, for instance, in failure to provide resources and/or to pursue suitable policies. Thus it may be agreed that EUR 50 is to be made available for each pupil; an added incentive to encourage girls in particular might be an agreement on an increased amount for each female pupil.

If RBA approaches are to work, reliable indicators and appropriate (regularly collected) data as well as accurately defined targets (results) are needed. As quantifiable and measurable indicators are decisive for the success of RBA, sectors in which the aim is to provide services are particularly suitable; this is true of the social sectors, but also of the supply of, say, water and energy to households. In other areas (such as decentralisation and public financial management) the requirements in the form of indicators, measurement methods and so on are more difficult, but they can be met by means of adjustments in individual cases.

There are RBA proposals for a good number of areas, ranging from the performance-oriented shaping of budget support instruments (for example, the variable tranches of EU budget support) to approaches that seek to achieve a specific result in a given sector (for example, the number of school-leavers).

2   **Results-based financing (RBF)** consists in a contractual relationship within a partner country. The debate on such approaches began in OECD countries under the heading "New Public Management". The contractual relationship is established between, say, a ministry and a service provider (civil society groups, a health centre or something similar), who is required to provide certain services. The goal may be, for example, to increase the rate of medically attended births. If, say, the cost of transport to medical facilities is a major problem in this context, transport vouchers for pregnant women may remove a serious obstacle.

DOI: 10.1057/9781137397881.0010

BOX 4.2   *Incentive-based services*

RBF activities have been supported by donors (such as the World Bank, DFID and German development cooperation) on a major scale for years (see, Grittner 2013). The areas of application are to be found primarily in the social sectors and basic infrastructure. The activities include, for example, conditional payments to target groups. It is agreed with them that they will use certain services (in the health sector, for example); in return they will receive a certain sum of money. Another form may consist in service providers being offered incentives to provide certain services of an agreed quality (Output-Based Aid (OBA), Pay for Performance (P4P), Performance-Based Contracting and so on). The service providers then receive a fixed amount for each beneficiary or each unit of service (for example, the maintenance of one kilometre of roadway), for example.

Although both approaches are based on the same rationale (incentive effects), the levels of intervention differ fundamentally: while RBA concerns a relationship between donor and recipient (the incentive system is meant to motivate the partner to pursue a policy with which to achieve the results), the second approach concerns a contractual relationship between the principal (for example, one of the partner country's ministries) and the actual service provider. The aim here is to offer a sufficiently attractive incentive for the service to be provided. In individual cases, the two approaches can be combined, but this is not imperative.

4.1.1   What advantages and disadvantages can RBA approaches have?

There has so far been little practical experience of RBA approaches (see, Klingebiel 2012c). In the area of budget support, the EU has for some years been using an RBA-type instrument in what are known as variable tranches, which are based on performance agreements. The result indicators used in this context relate in particular to the health, education and water sectors. Experience of performance-based tranches in major budget support approaches has been positive, since an incremental payment procedure makes development aid inflows predictable to some extent and acts as a performance incentive. The USA's Millennium

Challenge Corporation (MCC) programme similarly adopts a results-based approach in that the instrument may be used only for countries meeting the requirements set out in a list of indicators. The United Kingdom's DFID is currently preparing results-based projects in a fairly small group of African countries, mostly for the education sector. In 2011 the World Bank added Program-for-Results Financing, a results-based approach, to its set of instruments.

Potential advantages and disadvantages of approaches of which little practical experience has yet been gained can be identified. This is true, for example, of the Cash on Delivery approach developed by the Centre for Global Development (money on production of evidence of practical results) (see, Birdsall / Savedoff 2010) and similar approaches.

The advantages may include the following:

▶ *Action is geared directly to results*: The action taken by both actors (donor and partner government) is largely determined by the results pursued. The links between development cooperation projects and results become closer (because of the incentive effect).

▶ *Relevance of incentives*: The contribution made by development cooperation is a strong incentive to the partner country to do what is necessary.

▶ *Increase in the partner's responsibility for implementation*: It is for the partner government to achieve the results. As the donors bear no responsibility for implementation, the partner's systems are strengthened.

▶ *Better evidence of development cooperation results*: The "attribution gap" (which occurs when results cannot be causally linked to the development aid) can be better closed in individual cases. This may help donors to show their own public the practical benefits of development cooperation (visibility of the development partner); however, "automatic attribution" is not possible in this case, either.

Disadvantages or limitations may exist in the following (and other) respects (see, Klingebiel 2012c; Pereira / Villota 2012):

▶ *Susceptibility of the partner system to performance incentives*: The concept presupposes that the partner is susceptible to performance incentives. This applies to the group of partner countries that tend to be good performers or at least have certain capable institutions (pockets of effectiveness).

DOI: 10.1057/9781137397881.0010

▶ *Disincentives, unintended effects and non-systemic action*: As a general rule, disincentives entail risks; focusing heavily on individual results tends to give rise to a non-systemic analysis and approach. Heavy pressure to achieve results may, for example, lead to other tasks in a sector being neglected. The risk with indicators that are perhaps not really suitable is that a policy overly geared to quantitative results is pursued. If, say, only the number of pupils leaving the school system was recorded as the result, there would be a danger of serious losses of quality in the education system (increase in pupil numbers per class and so on). Another question is whether the partner country's processes are not undermined by the effects of the incentive (the budget priorities set by the parliament, for example).

▶ *Capacities*: The approach presupposes that the partner has the capacities needed to achieve the results. If the partner's capacities and the public financial management system are inadequate, it may be unrealistic to believe the results can be achieved.

▶ *Sectors and data*: Results-based approaches cannot be adopted to good effect in all sectors alike. Conditions in such social sectors as health and education and sectors with easily measurable infrastructure performance (transport, household water supply and so on) are relatively good. In other areas some results are more difficult to measure or to agree with the partner (as in some areas of good governance), and the direct effects cannot always be assigned to one level of results. Moreover, the approach may help a major incentive to manipulate data to develop.

▶ *De-coupling of (some) RBA approaches from their political context/ omission of policy dialogue*: RBA approaches that provide for automatic payment on the achievement of results may give rise, in unfavourable circumstances, to a situation in which a development partner is obliged to make payments despite serious governance problems (such as widespread violations of human rights).

▶ *Inadequate advance financing capacity*: The approach provides for the partner to finance the project in advance. This may become a serious obstacle for low-income countries because of their limited room for budgetary manoeuvre. However, start-up financing models are conceivable.

▶ *Time-horizon*: If results can be achieved only in the medium or longer term, short-term political factors (parliamentary terms and

DOI: 10.1057/9781137397881.0010

so on) may favour projects that produce early results. RBA then encourages a short-term perspective.

Against the background of the international debate, the following conclusions are important: first, results-based approaches embrace an extremely wide range of instruments and lines of action. A simple, but important distinction can be made between (i) results-based aid approaches and (ii) results-based financing approaches. Second, existing instruments already make it easy for performance incentives to be offered. This is true, for instance, of the division of budget support into variable tranches. Third, practical experience of other RBA approaches (such as Cash on Delivery) has yet to be gained. There is some legitimate fear in this case that the disadvantages (especially disincentives) will outweigh the advantages. Pilot projects should be run so that it can be seen not only whether RBA approaches are possible in principle, but also whether they achieve more than other aid approaches. Fourth, the hoped-for political benefit of some RBA approaches, namely the ability to produce accurate evidence of results, is, in some respects at least, a chimera. The links between effects are, as a general rule, complex, and unintended effects must also be taken into account. Lastly, RBA approaches presuppose the partner's clear orientation towards performance, which is true of the group of dynamically reforming countries (good performers). This means that the very countries facing the greatest challenges cannot be reached.

DOI: 10.1057/9781137397881.0010

5
Effectiveness: What Does Development Cooperation Achieve?

Abstract: *Since the early 2000s a greater interest has been taken in the question of how to arrange development cooperation so that it is more effective The Paris Declaration plays a central role in international efforts to increase the effectiveness of aid. It seeks to reduce the number of weak points that stand in the way of more effective aid, such as donor instruments that are geared primarily to the interests of the donors' structures, and their partners' unwillingness or inability to manage development cooperation processes. Self-interest has so far prevented the donors in particular from implementing any more than a few aspects of the principles agreed in Paris.*

Klingebiel, Stephan. *Development Cooperation: Challenges of the New Aid Architecture.* Basingstoke: Palgrave Macmillan, 2014. DOI: 10.1057/9781137397881.0011.

DOI: 10.1057/9781137397881.0011

5.1   The debate on the effects and effectiveness of development cooperation

Successful development in partner countries depends on a wide range of factors, particularly important among them being their own policies. This is most apparent where poor governance increases a country's fragility and/or leads to violent conflict. Internal policies can prevent people from earning a living or social services from being available – even though a country may have extensive resources. This becomes particularly visible in the case of countries with high incomes from oil revenues: where governance is poor, better living conditions do not automatically follow. External factors may also lead to the success or failure of development, by giving or denying access to markets in developed regions, for instance. Overfishing by international fishing fleets (from the EU, say) is an example of international activities being to blame for the fact that people in developing countries can no longer earn a living. Aid may also bring about successful development. This is especially true of countries that are particularly poor and dependent on development aid. Much effort has therefore gone into attempts to make such aid as effective as possible. The ability of development aid to shape events should not be overestimated, however: other policies and conditions also play their part.

The effectiveness of development aid is debated at international level from two angles in particular: first, a debate has been going on for decades over whether development aid achieves anything at all. Second, since the early 2000s a greater interest has been taken in the question of how to arrange development aid so that it is more effective. The debate particularly concerns international aid effectiveness standards.

Effects of development aid

Evidence of the effects of development aid is essentially discussed at two levels.

The first level turns on the question whether development aid can be shown to make a contribution to economic growth in developing countries. For this debate 2000 was a key year. On the basis of econometric comparisons of countries, a study by two World Bank authors (Burnside / Dollar 2000) concluded that development aid makes a demonstrable contribution to economic growth in countries which pursue "good policies".[1] The study had an enormous impact. The debate in the 2000s on the need for additional development aid resources

DOI: 10.1057/9781137397881.0011

was very largely based on these conclusions. Since then the academic debate has intensively discussed the causal links between growth and aid (Faust / Leiderer 2010). Critics question whether what appears to be a plausible proposition is capable of constantly standing the empirical test (see, Easterly 2003; Temple 2010; Radelet 2006). And indeed, generally accepted evidence of development aid making a positive contribution to economic growth has yet to be presented.

The second level concerns evidence of effects that projects may or may not have. Donor organisations regularly present extensive material (evaluations and so on) intended to prove that their development aid projects have had positive effects. In the academic debate, reference is made in this context to a "micro-macro paradox" (see, Boone 1996; Temple 2010), since it is often impossible to reconcile the favourable results with the overall situation in the country concerned: if all the positive effects had actually occurred, it should also be possible to find empirical evidence of them at country or sectoral level. Frequently, this is not the case.

BOX 5.1   *How much development through aid?*

Sub-Saharan Africa's economic situation has developed positively in the past twenty years, largely due to better policies. Some 10 to 20 countries in the region have managed to achieve significant growth rates, despite the international economic crisis. But economic dynamism is still unsatisfactory in many countries where, despite growth, there has been less than adequate improvement in living conditions. Reforms aimed at improving the political environment have yet to be undertaken in many countries. What is behind the recent progress? Was international aid possibly more successful than many have conjectured? And what does that mean for the future role of aid in Africa?

Aid continues to play an important role, even with increasing foreign direct investment and remittances. With China and other new actors, the importance of South-South relations for sub-Saharan Africa is growing. In large part, success stories about economic progress have dominated international coverage of Sub-Saharan Africa in recent years. This attention is justified, since the situation of these 48 countries has continued to take on clearer outlines.

DOI: 10.1057/9781137397881.0011

The countries of sub-Saharan Africa have undergone processes of change at different speeds and, to some extent, in different directions. Existing country classifications have only just begun to find appropriate categories for the current process of differentiation. In fact, some countries in the region – though not all – can look back on an economic success story that has been going on for several years. By and large, sub-Saharan Africa's economic situation has developed positively in the past twenty years, not least because the various countries have pursued better policies.

The question, of course, is: what is behind the progress made by some African countries in the last one to two decades? Was international support for the continent in the form of development cooperation possibly more successful than many have conjectured? And what does that mean for the future role of aid in the region?

An impact hard to define

There is no really accurate and reliable way of measuring the contribution that aid makes to successful development. What is clear, however, is that the policies of the countries themselves are decisive in many respects. Countries which have successfully reduced the number of poor people in their populations and have initiated growth processes (that is, those not totally reliant on natural resources) have been able to do so on the basis of their comparatively good governance activities.

It makes a great deal of difference, for example, whether clientelistic structures predominate in a country or transparent processes determine how public resources are used. In much the same way, the international context is also important for African countries, which are being increasingly drawn into the processes of globalisation.

The interest of such emerging economies as China and India in African countries is partly responsible for the traditional European and North American cooperation partners shifting their focus. All this means that, for African states too, many factors influence policies, aid being only one of them.

Variances in development

The importance of the "aid factor" in this regard varies. On the whole, political obligations within the G8 context and in other fora

DOI: 10.1057/9781137397881.0011

have led to substantial growth of aid to sub-Saharan Africa in the last 10 to 15 years. Some US$ 44 billion is provided by OECD donors annually.

A number of countries are very dependent on aid funds for their public investments. In some cases, such as Burundi, considerably more than 20 per cent of a country's entire economic power is tied to aid. In other cases, such as Angola and South Africa, aid has gradually shrunk until it is now of marginal importance, amounting to far less than 1 per cent of GDP.

The numbers for these countries show that flows of private funds to the sub-Saharan African region have now risen to a much higher level than aid. This steep rise has been accompanied by major changes to financial structures, the proportion of private inflows having increased significantly.

Aid continues to play an important role, although the scene is increasingly dominated by foreign direct investment and migrant workers' remittances. Such "new cooperation partners" as China, India and Arab countries are also triggering major changes; the importance of South-South relations for sub-Saharan Africa is growing.

In the coming years, the trend in sub-Saharan Africa is likely to continue assuming a clearer outline. The reasons: on the one hand, aid will be increasingly sidelined by a steadily growing group of countries. Countries undergoing dynamic reform will focus even more on the private sector and foreign direct investment than they do today.

For other countries, now in the grip of an oil and minerals boom, the primary question is whether available resources will benefit the population at large. Nigeria and other countries offer an abundance of study material for the much discussed "curse of resources".

On the other hand, some countries in the region will remain dependent on aid for the foreseeable future. In fragile countries, aid and humanitarian assistance are often of crucial importance for the maintenance of a minimum of state structures and public services.

Aside from this, however, there are numerous poor countries – such as Ethiopia – which are entirely functional, but for which aid will continue to be an important means of financing and implementing long-term programmes that address poverty and growth. But even such low-income countries as Liberia and Rwanda are making growing efforts to escape their long dependence on aid.

DOI: 10.1057/9781137397881.0011

The Paris Agenda

The Paris Declaration is of prime importance for international efforts to increase aid effectiveness (see, Ashoff 2010b). It attempts to reduce the weaknesses that stand in the way of more effective aid, such as donor instruments geared primarily to the interests of donor structures and partners' unwillingness or inability to manage development cooperation processes. The Declaration was adopted in 2005 by representatives of developing, emerging and industrialised countries and refers to five basic principles:

1. Partner countries to take more responsibility (*ownership*) for their policies and development strategies and to coordinate all development measures.
2. Increased *alignment* with and use of partner countries' systems (for example, donors' use of partners' budgets and audit offices).
3. Increased *harmonisation* and coordination among donors.
4. *Managing for development results*.
5. Improved *mutual accountability* of donors and partners.

The Paris Declaration promised to become an effective approach because it succeeded in linking the principles to measurable quality indicators. One of the main weaknesses of development cooperation and other areas of international cooperation is that, although actors find it relatively easy to agree on general principles – such as closer coordination – their action is often subject to other principles. The harmonisation of donor activities, for example, has often failed because of donors' limited willingness to abandon their own standards (to meet the control requirements of their own audit offices, for instance). Another example is the use of the partner's national systems, donor organisations often having an interest in having their own personnel implement projects. This frequently prevents the partner country from deriving maximum benefit (best available quality for the best possible price) from development projects. That benefit would be gained if, say, consultancy projects were freely advertised. The indicators in the Paris Declaration address these main issues.

Evaluations of the application of the five Paris principles and the 56 specific commitments show that, although the tendency is generally positive (as in the case of aid transparency), the agreed goals have not yet been achieved, especially by donors (Wood et al. 2011).

DOI: 10.1057/9781137397881.0011

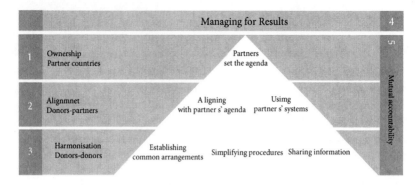

FIGURE 5.1   *The Paris Declaration pyramid – five shared principles*
Source: OECD (2011b, 18).

The Paris Declaration was followed by two further high-level meetings, one held in Accra in 2008 (Accra Agenda for Action), the other in Busan in 2011 (Busan Partnership for Effective Development Co-operation). In Busan "new actors" (especially China) were more heavily involved in the "effectiveness agenda", and the term "aid effectiveness" was replaced by "development effectiveness" to reflect the fact that, besides aid, a number of other policies of donors and partners are important if development is to make progress. These policies are to be examined more closely for the contribution they make to development.

BOX 5.2   *Two-speed aid effectiveness*[2]

The Busan summit (29.11.2011–01.12.2011), which almost came to nothing because of China's temporary refusal to sign the final declaration, had a fundamental dilemma to resolve. The first challenge was to maintain the momentum of the effectiveness agenda of the previous years. The previous two high-level meetings, held in Paris (2005) and Accra (2008) with the aim of improving aid effectiveness, had actually achieved results in that the aid partners had entered into mutual and, above all, verifiable commitments. The donors in particular are, however, finding it difficult to honour those commitments when, for example, it comes to partner countries themselves being responsible for implementation, rather than the donors' agencies.

The second challenge was to involve new actors. What is true of many international issues is also true of development policy: the

DOI: 10.1057/9781137397881.0011

environment changes rapidly, possibly more rapidly than the political actors are able to find appropriate responses. For development cooperation these changes consist not least in the fact that many new donors – the economically successful Asian countries and private foundations (such as the Bill and Melinda Gates Foundation) – are gaining in importance and reducing the weight carried by the old OECD donor group appreciably, even in financial terms. For understandable reasons the new actors do not want simply to endorse the commitments and procedures which they see as being dominated by traditional donors. Accordingly, the aim in Busan was to integrate these new actors and relationships effectively into an effectiveness agenda with a future.

In the language of European integration policy this twofold objective might be construed as a dilemma between "deepening" and "widening". What was the Busan meeting able to achieve in these circumstances? The results can be interpreted as the design for a new international development aid architecture. The approach is based less on a self-contained plan showing how a future structure might look, offering, instead, pointers to how debates on more effective aid should be conducted in the future. There are signs that there will be "two speeds" in the future. The group of donors wanting to continue to abide closely by the Paris and Accra commitments and to implement and advance the present agenda for more effective aid with great dedication would be the "fast group". The United Kingdom is the prime advocate of this fast pace, although this erstwhile aid paragon has lost some of its pace and sparkle in recent years. Certain statements in the Busan Declaration therefore concern only signatories who have already been involved in the past.

The second group of donors, on the other hand, does not see itself bound by past and present pledges, or only partly so. There may be various reasons for this. Such new donors as Brazil, India and China can claim with some justification that the aid discussion fora reflect the old "North-South structures" and modernisation efforts hitherto have not been all that convincing. To this second group might be added, in practice, those donors – such as France, the USA and Japan – who have had difficulty implementing the present aid effectiveness agenda.

The results of the Busan meeting allow for two different interpretations. First, the optimistic view: the participants succeeded in

DOI: 10.1057/9781137397881.0011

outlining in the final declaration a new, broader development partnership which includes the new actors and new cooperative relationships, without releasing the signatories of the Paris/Accra agenda from their commitments. The signatories explicitly undertake, for example, to continue honouring their respective commitments. At the same time, the Busan final document sets out a number of new, "softer" principles that enable the new actors to join the consensus. A pragmatic, but important first move has thus been made to take these actors "on board" and lock them into a broader effectiveness agenda. This applies not only to the new actors from the South, but also to the governments of the industrialised countries, which have hitherto been restrained in their reaction to the Paris/Accra agenda or, after changes of government in Europe in recent years, have sought, politically at least, to put some distance between themselves and the commitments entered into by their predecessors.

Second, the sceptical view: The transition from the concept of more effective aid to that of broad-based development effectiveness is the "scent mark" of the Busan declaration. The parties to the agreement are aware that aid can represent only a small proportion of the efforts to achieve sustainable development in partner countries. Other policies and approaches must therefore be designed to gain maximum benefit for development. This idea is as simple as it is right. Nonetheless, it cannot be said with any certainty that progress is then bound to follow. As regards the Paris and Accra commitments, it has become apparent that, although good and verifiable agreements were reached, they are not being adequately implemented. In this situation, is it in the interests of a broader-based new global partnership for the pressure on the donors to do their homework to be eased?

Whether the optimistic or the sceptical view of the results achieved in Busan is more appropriate largely depends on the new aid architecture that is still emerging. A combination of the two main concerns – "deepening" and "widening" – has yet to be achieved.

5.2   What does effectiveness depend on?

For several decades it has been internationally agreed that the donor community should set aside 0.7 per cent of GNI for development

DOI: 10.1057/9781137397881.0011

cooperation. The donor group has repeatedly committed itself politically (in the form of G8 decisions and an EU step-by-step plan, for example) to increase resources for development cooperation significantly (see, Klingebiel 2010). The question is therefore: if the scale of development cooperation could be increased, can the effects be increased on roughly the same scale? Can it be shown that 0.7 per cent is an appropriate target? Would 0.9 per cent possibly be more appropriate, or would 0.5 per cent perhaps be better?

It is impossible to set an objectifiable quantitative figure for the optimum scale of aid transfers or for a country's aid requirements. As for the magnitude of the aid provided by all donors, a target of this kind is an unsuitable indicator, since it is no more than a very rough input figure for the sum of all developing countries.

If such an order of magnitude is not to be found at the level of all aid transfers, it must be asked whether it is possible at the level of individual countries or groups of countries. Various studies assume that there is a certain aid level above which the additional benefit (marginal utility) declines or the effect is even reversed. The first euros of aid thus have (above a critical mass) more effects than any further euros. Some analyses identify a "saturation point" above which added aid resources no longer make sense. This saturation point is not determined uniformly and is assumed to be between about 15 and 45 per cent of gross national income. The wide range demonstrates that no saturation point universally is yet applicable in practice; in fact, the figures differ widely even at the level of individual countries (Klingebiel 2006a). It is doubtful that such a figure can be usefully identified for all countries. The appropriate use of aid depends not only on its scale, but also on other aspects, which are discussed below. Why should a country with a comparatively poorly functioning administration be able to absorb the same amount of aid as a neighbouring country with a well-functioning administration? The situation is different again in countries that have just overcome violent conflict and are unable to raise much money of their own for the reconstruction of the transport infrastructure that has been destroyed. A situation of this nature is hardly comparable with that of countries with a long and uninterrupted history of aid. They are likely to need less for the financing of infrastructure. Absorptive capacity is, after all, linked to the use of resources. Aid inflows for the reduction of a balance-of-payments deficit, for example, are far easier to absorb than aid intended for the expansion of the supply of basic social services.

DOI: 10.1057/9781137397881.0011

That there is an albeit variable marginal utility has, on the other hand, been proved by quantitative and qualitative studies. If there is a point above which the benefit of aid declines sharply or is even reversed in its totality, the question is what mechanisms cause such an effect. Several areas of effects can be distinguished (Klingebiel 2006a).

5.2.1   Macroeconomic aspects

The effect that has been debated most concerns the danger of what is known as the Dutch disease.[3] This term describes the paradox of economies suddenly growing – primarily because of the discovery and production of natural resources – and then being confronted with serious macroeconomic problems. The trade surpluses due to the export of the natural resources cause the exchange rate to rise. This leads to marketing problems for other goods, which become less competitive and so more difficult to export. The gravity of the disease largely depends on the degree to which the available resources are used to finance additional imports or non-tradable goods (wages and salaries and so on). As the additional money supply may have inflationary effects, major problems may arise for the private sector in countries with poorly functioning financial markets (owing to erratic interest rate movements, for example). Country studies (of Ghana, Ethiopia, Uganda and so on) show that the adverse effects can be partly counteracted, but aid-dependent countries are limited in their capacity to cope with such challenges.

5.2.2   Governance and institutions

Heavy aid dependence or growing aid inflows may also have major effects on dimensions of governance and the quality of institutions in partner countries. These effects take many forms:

1   A substantial inflow of ODA may weaken national efforts to mobilise resources (Braeutigam / Knack 2004). This is true primarily of the development and practical use of tax-raising instruments. Canvassing for aid is an alternative to the collection of taxes; it does not need to be imposed against existing interests (privileged elites and so on).

2   Substantial aid inflows may undermine the partner government's accountability to its own people (Moss et al. 2006). If a large proportion of the investments in the country stems from donors

and many services are financed or provided by them, important political negotiating and decision-making processes take place between donors and partner governments, parliaments play only a small role in public budgets and reform programmes are negotiated and adopted with the donor community rather than representatives of society, the country's political economy is affected and the partner government's accountability to its own people is weakened. The extent to which such negative side-effects actually occur largely depends on the aid modalities. If the partner's structures are used and its parliament plays a role in the decision-making, adverse effects may be avoided and the partner's systems strengthened. The situation is more difficult where aid by-passes structures and processes in the partner country.

3   Aid inflows may encourage the emergence of rentier states (see, Collier 2006b). Revenue from the exploitation of natural resources (such as oil in the Middle East) may ease the pressure on elites to democratise political systems and introduce accountable procedures. Aid inflows may have a comparable effect.

4   Substantial government and administration capacities may be tied up in communication with donors and in project- or programme-related procedures (reporting obligations, missions and so on). A large proportion of the donor's capacities is then devoted to its structures (see, Klingebiel / Leiderer / Schmidt 2007).

5   If aid structures replace the role of the partner, they may undermine government capacities. Added to this, aid systems may have an adverse incentive effect on public servants, especially in countries with particularly weak structures. Donor offices usually pay higher salaries and so entice personnel away from partner structures; this is especially true of highly qualified staff. Considerable additional income can be obtained from "attendance allowances" and training courses at home and abroad; performance incentives are created outside national administrations (Moss et al. 2006).

6   Heavy state dependence on ODA significantly increases the risk of a coup d'état, according to Paul Collier (2006a). He ascribes this risk to the "honeypot" effect, which makes government posts attractive as a source of income. African governments have typically reacted to this risk by raising military spending, a large proportion of which has in turn been funded indirectly by aid because of the fungibility effect.

DOI: 10.1057/9781137397881.0011

BOX 5.3   *Fungibility of aid*

Aid is described as fungible when it enables the partner country to reduce its own expenditure for the intended purpose. The resources saved can then be used for another purpose. Neither project-related nor sector-specific approaches can exclude the fungibility problem. Aid made available to a country for the construction of schools, for instance, may result in the amount concerned being saved in the partner country's budget or spent elsewhere (in the education or other sectors). The degree to which the fungibility effect contributes to the failure to spend all or part of the aid on development priorities depends on the specific circumstances in the individual case. Empirical studies reveal a wide variety of effects (see, Leiderer 2012a; Temple 2010). Whether aid resources are used fungibly can be determined only through studies of the whole budget procedure.

5.2.3   Accountability and aid effectiveness

Accountability and rendering account are of considerable interest in the context of the debate on more effective development cooperation (see, de Renzio 2006). In general terms, accountability is the obligation on a person, group or institution to justify their decisions and actions to another person, group or institution. It is linked to sanctions for fulfilment or non-fulfilment and is therefore based on incentives.

In the development cooperation context, accountability is relevant in three respects:

▸ accountability in the donor country;
▸ accountability in partner countries (domestic accountability);
▸ mutual accountability of partners and donors.

Donors[4] and partner countries are accountable in particular to parliaments, the electorate, civil society, the media and national audit offices.

In the debate on more effective aid (that is, the Paris Declaration, the Accra Agenda for Action and the Busan Partnership document) mutual accountability and accountability to the actual target groups in partner countries play an especially important role.

Challenges and problems

The forms of accountability referred to above are not necessarily complementary. In some cases, they may even compete with one another

DOI: 10.1057/9781137397881.0011

(see, de Renzio 2006; Klingebiel 2012c). Challenges exist particularly in the following areas:

▸ In the past the (implicit) emphasis lay on the accountability of aid recipients to donors. This has undergone a conceptual change, particularly with the debates on aid effectiveness (Paris Declaration and so on); the implementation of new conceptions, however, has yet to be completed.

▸ This donor-related focus impairs the effectiveness of aid (owing to risk aversion, the circumvention of national systems, "project islands", the donor's implementation interests and so on).

▸ Accountability in partner countries often comes up against inadequately functioning structures: parliaments are weak, the media hardly capable of playing the role of the "fourth estate". Partner governments do not necessarily have any interest in functioning accountability systems in their own countries, since they may lead to calls for governance reforms.

▸ Mutual accountability is sometimes expensive, compromise-laden and afflicted with deficiencies. This is as true of coordinated national development strategies as it is of joint monitoring approaches and policy analyses.

Prospects

It is possible to identify a number of approaches to strengthening accountability in the development cooperation context. Functioning public financial management systems (including budget planning processes and checks on the use of resources) are legitimate concerns of partner countries and their actors themselves. The aid effectiveness principles therefore wisely focus on partner countries' national systems; this gives greater weight not least to parliaments, civil society actors and so on. On the donors' side there is still much room for improvement. Development cooperation can help to strengthen accountability systems and to reduce unintended weakening effects. External actors are better able to support the "supply" of accountability, less able to endorse the "demand" for it.

Donors are legitimately concerned about accountability in their own countries. Such accountability is essential if they are to receive political and societal backing for the provision of public resources for development tasks. When it comes to rendering account, a distinction needs to be made between, on the one hand, sometimes complex and often

DOI: 10.1057/9781137397881.0011

abstract development cooperation systems and effect chains (in which donor administrations and parliamentary select committees should be especially interested) and, on the other hand, the need for transparency and the dissemination of information to a wider public.

Results-based approaches in development cooperation may strengthen mutual and domestic accountability, since they are based on the implementation of the partner's policies and activities; this may also relate to monitoring and evaluation (M&E) systems, which are very important for accountability. There is a wide range of results-based approaches, but there may be risks associated with them as a result, for instance, of disincentives or concentration on activities that can be quantified.

BOX 5.4   *Decentralisation, public financial management and development aid*

The ongoing trend of decentralising governance responsibilities to the subnational level in many countries of sub-Saharan Africa is likely to continue in the near future. If it is to achieve its objectives, it will be crucial that this transfer of responsibilities is matched by equal efforts to increase subnational Public Financial Management (PFM) capacities.

As a cross-cutting issue of domestic accountability systems and of development policy, PFM lies at the heart of countries' governance systems. It therefore comes as no surprise that PFM systems at central government level have become one of the key reform areas in developing countries in sub-Saharan Africa. At the same time, however, the capacity of and the conditions for PFM at the subnational tiers of government have to date received far less attention. While there are signs of a growing demand for subnational PFM approaches, development partners have not yet fully come to terms with the implications of this trend when designing their technical and financial support programmes.

Importance of subnational PFM reforms

In all developing and developed regions PFM is a core dimension of governance, which includes not only technical systems and processes, but wider issues of institutions and incentives. The ultimate objective of PFM reforms is to achieve more transparent, more

DOI: 10.1057/9781137397881.0011

effective and more efficient management of government revenue, expenditure, assets and liabilities. Well-functioning PFM systems are vital for all countries: they are needed to implement policies in all sectors effectively and efficiently.

Good PFM systems in a number of sub-Saharan African countries will also attract additional donors willing to use national systems, they will give domestic and foreign investors confidence in the sustainability of government finances, and they will help countries to gain earlier and better access to international capital markets. Governance reforms that focus on decentralisation depend on well-functioning and robust PFM systems at subnational level.

Of late, countries in sub-Saharan Africa have been touting their economic growth potential, and available resources may increase further, which will again require functioning PFM systems at subnational as well as national level. Against this background, there is much support for the claim that subnational PFM reforms are particularly important for and relevant to development cooperation. At the same time, the topic seems to have been under-researched in the past.

Assessing subnational PFM in sub-Saharan Africa

Motivation for decentralisation also varies. In some countries and regions, decentralisation is associated with the process of overall political and economic transformation. In other countries, it is linked to the process of democratisation. Sometimes, the main aim of decentralisation is to eliminate conditions conducive to conflict (for example, through the inclusion of local communities); in other cases, its aim is the improvement of service delivery to the people.

Conditions under which decentralisation takes place – including population size and geographical conditions – also differ widely from country to country. Research shows, in some crucial areas at least, decentralisation efforts make positive contributions to the development process (for example, through the provision of basic services and participation in local politics).

Since 2005, the PEFA *(Public Expenditure and Financial Accountability)* framework has made a significant contribution to the streamlining and consolidation of assessment efforts. During this period, PEFA has established itself as an internationally recognised

DOI: 10.1057/9781137397881.0011

analytical tool and the "global standard" for assessing primarily national PFM systems.

The number of assessments of PFM systems at subnational level with the *PEFA* framework is rising fast. Interestingly, the majority of subnational assessments have been undertaken in the sub-Saharan Africa region. The group of "early adopters" and, subsequently, "heavy users" of the PEFA framework at subnational level in sub-Saharan Africa – namely, the large federal states of Ethiopia and Nigeria – have been joined by other countries in the region – such as Rwanda – where decentralisation efforts began more recently.

What is different about PFM systems at subnational level?

Subnational PFM systems have some characteristics that distinguish them from the central government level:

- *Subnational revenue:* In most countries of sub-Saharan Africa, the existing legal framework gives the national government a dominant role in the collection of taxes and other revenue. Resource mobilisation also tends to be subject to widespread capacity constraints. As a result, public revenue at subnational level remains limited, and fiscal transfers from central levels constitute the main source of revenue. Subnational governments also typically do not have the authority to borrow to cover short- or long-term financing gaps.
- *Planning and budgeting:* Given their more limited scope and capacities, it must be realised that subnational development plans and budgets rarely reach the level of sophistication to be found at central government level. For example, if they are included at all, macroeconomic analysis, revenue forecasts and so on are frequently adopted from the higher level. Central government normally retains planning and budgeting authority for national roads, for example, as some subnational entities may be discouraged from investing in good roads if they will be mainly used by traffic from outside their own jurisdiction. While government at subnational level generally relies on the central level to function as a "policy compass", it often does not engage in medium-term planning processes, limiting itself to taking no more than an annual view. The budgeting process at subnational level can therefore generally be seen as a function

DOI: 10.1057/9781137397881.0011

of the central process. Finally, the costing of services, which can pose a challenge even to much more advanced central government planning departments, is a particularly difficult area for the subnational level, as is budgeting for operations and maintenance.

– *Budget execution and procurement:* Challenges in budget execution primarily occur among activities financed by discretionary funds managed at subnational level. They frequently result from unpredictable allocations, unrealistic or excessive conditionality in the case of earmarked transfers, challenges arising in subnational procurement processes that cause delays and general capacity issues. Finally, external conditions at subnational level – such as the distance from the centre, fewer opportunities for staff advancement and so on – can sometimes put an additional strain on subnational PFM capacities, with the "best and brightest" budget officers seeking employment elsewhere.

– *Internal control:* The mechanisms, instruments and methods of subnational accountability frameworks are generally defined in legal texts or a country's decentralisation strategy, with differences resulting from the specific characteristics and requirements of the subnational level. In terms of internal control, subnational legislatures that work only part-time and have less support capacity at their disposal are frequently at a structural disadvantage by comparison with central government institutions.

– *Accounting and reporting:* Countries of sub-Saharan Africa that have unitary systems generally have unitary accounting standards for both the central and the subnational level. On the other hand, some subnational entities in decentralised states also have the power to define and use their own accounting and reporting rules. From a subnational perspective, the benefits of comprehensiveness – including the classification of a budget in terms of poverty/non-poverty relevance or according to different government spending programmes – must be offset against the additional PFM and administrative burdens imposed, for which capacities are limited. The swift reconciliation of bank accounts, which is a key PFM issue in this respect, is frequently hampered by distance/connectivity

DOI: 10.1057/9781137397881.0011

issues between cost centres and the lack of banking facilities at subnational level.
  – *External control:* For the subnational level, the external audit function may be assigned to an audit institution at local level, or it may remain a central government function, or the responsibility may be shared to some extent, for example by function, geography or institutional coverage. A clear-cut division of labour between the subnational level and central government ("who audits what?") becomes a crucial precondition for a functioning external accountability mechanism. Depending on their specific comparative advantages, differentiation based on specific functional requirements – financial audits and performance/value-for-money audits, for example – is also possible.

What are the implications for development partners?

A number of implications and conclusions for development partners can be derived from an analysis of the subnational PFM characteristics and requirements set out above.

First, it must be recognised that supporting subnational PFM capacities and functions is not only beneficial from the narrow technical perspective of improving the management of domestic and donor funds, but may also have positive externalities from a governance perspective (see, Klingebiel / Mahn, 2011). The positive implications of revenue generation through taxation – which results in the direct improvement of public services at that level – for citizen-state relationships are but one example.

Second, direct donor support for the subnational level – irrespective of its form – must be so implemented that the distribution of government resources is not skewed. In a number of countries, central government has adopted rules and practices for "offsetting" direct donor support for the subnational level with a corresponding reduction in their own support. In these cases, delays in donor support reaching the subnational level may result in additional challenges for the subnational government, particularly when it does not have access to short-term borrowing.

Third, the variety of systems and conditions at subnational level makes monitoring and evaluation reforms of the PFM systems using the PEFA framework a challenge. The PEFA Steering Committee

DOI: 10.1057/9781137397881.0011

might want to consider further developments of the framework for its application at subnational level.

Fourth, given the even greater scope for dissimilarities and differences of "stages" of decentralisation, the need to contextualise PFM reforms at subnational level is arguably even greater than at central government level. PFM reforms at central government level often seem to be focused on the implementation of sophisticated systems at the expense of the search for simpler, more user-friendly and robust alternatives. This is partly due to the perception that it is necessary for PFM systems in SSA to conform to international best practices and to the emphasis on ensuring that demanding reform packages are aligned with the development partners' incentive structure and "business model".

Finally, coordination between the subnational and the central government level on PFM issues and, in particular, the respective reforms are vital. There are numerous examples of subnational PFM reforms that do not comply with requirements at the centre, and vice versa. Bridging the gap between decentralisation and PFM research and reform efforts has a significant contribution to make in this respect.

Source: Klingebiel / Mahn (2013)

Notes

1   Burnside and Dollar were reacting to some partly critical analyses published in the latter half of the 1990s, especially that by Peter Boone (1996).
2   Box 6 is based, with some minor amendments, on Klingebiel / Leiderer (2011).
3   The term emerged in the context of the discovery of new gas reserves in the Netherlands in the 1960s. This was followed by an upward revaluation of the Dutch guilder and a decline in industrial production (see, Liebig / Ressel / Rondorf 2008; Temple 2010).
4   In the case of a bilateral donor; in the case of multilateral donors, the structure of accountability is sometimes arranged differently.

DOI: 10.1057/9781137397881.0011

6
Global Challenges and Development Cooperation

Abstract: *Proposals for changes to the management of global problems can be roughly divided into two categories: first, approaches that are outlined against a development background. They include various contributions that can be subsumed under the term "beyond aid". They are at pains to improve the development cooperation system further and to integrate it into other development efforts. Second, it is possible to identify conceptual designs relating to new models of international cooperation. This category includes, in particular, global governance research. For problem management, debates on global public goods have proved particularly fruitful in this context.*

Klingebiel, Stephan. *Development Cooperation: Challenges of the New Aid Architecture.* Basingstoke: Palgrave Macmillan, 2014. DOI: 10.1057/9781137397881.0012.

DOI: 10.1057/9781137397881.0012

Debates on the future of development cooperation assume that a highly dynamic environment will force it to adjust (see, Rogerson 2011; Kharas / Makino / Jung 2011). Various debates begin by focusing on the existing defects in the management of global challenges. On the whole, the treatment of global challenges at national, regional and global level is fragmented and deficient. Many actors are involved in development tasks. They are, however, working in a fragmented, uncoordinated system which is itself barely controllable, even when transaction costs are high. Furthermore, policies that influence developing countries are, in many areas, not sufficiently joined up or coherent. At present, the networking of global policies is still in its infancy, as is the adoption of approaches to overcoming conflicts of objectives (such as ecological sustainability versus resource consumption due to economic growth).

Proposals for changes to the management of global problems can be roughly divided into two categories: first, approaches that are outlined against a development background. They include various contributions that can be subsumed under the term "beyond aid". They are at pains to develop the development cooperation system further and to integrate it into other development efforts. Second, it is possible to identify conceptual designs relating to new models of international cooperation. This category includes, in particular, global governance research (for example, Messner / Nuscheler 2003). For problem management, debates on global public goods have proved particularly fruitful in this context.

6.1   Beyond aid

"Beyond aid" debates seek to overcome an aid-centred focus in cooperation with developing countries. This does not mean that these approaches dispute the need for aid or aid-like contributions.

Essentially, three lines of discussion can be distinguished:

▸ *Importance of partner countries' policies*: Debates on development cooperation are sometimes constricted. A distorted picture is painted of political responsibility for successful development, or its absence, because the importance of the various structures of responsibility in partner countries is underestimated and that of external actors and especially donors overrated. In favourable cases, development cooperation can benefit and support development

DOI: 10.1057/9781137397881.0012

processes. The decisive policies, reforms and changes that lead to "development" are, however, primarily the products of those responsible in the countries themselves (Kharas / Makino / Jung 2011). A distorted perception of the role of national actors may have various implications. The heavy dependence of a government on aid for its budgets and the action it takes may contribute to structural shortcomings in the country's political accountability. Governments can gear their accountability primarily to donors, with little or no regard for their own people (see, Vollmer 2012). The mobilisation of domestic resources, particularly in the form of taxes, is therefore important in terms not only of funds available, but also of governance structures. Consequently, the debate on beyond aid approaches examines the mobilisation of domestic resources and the associated effects on governance.

▶ *Catalytic function of development cooperation*: Development cooperation is based on the assumption that the contribution it makes complements that made by other development resources and that investment would otherwise not be effected or to only a limited degree. It is also assumed that aid has a mobilising effect on other financial sources. Development cooperation is thus meant to contribute to the crowding in of other resources, rather than their crowding out. Whether it actually has such a catalytic effect can hardly be proved in general or in specific cases. No recognised evidence of development cooperation making a general contribution to economic growth (that is, generating further resource inflows) has yet been presented; regression analyses, in fact, allow of contradictory interpretations (Barder 2011). Similarly unclear are the displacement, reinforcement and freeloading effects of individual investments and projects in which public and private actors engage (public-private partnerships) in development cooperation (Rogerson 2011).

▶ *Coherence of donor policies and international regimes*: The call for development policy coherence stems from the realisation that, besides development cooperation, there are other policies that influence the development of partner countries and are often more dominant in the influence they wield (as regards the extent to which a country is integrated into the world market, the structure of its foreign trade, the effects of foreign direct investment and so on). Stated "negatively", policy coherence

DOI: 10.1057/9781137397881.0012

means the absence of incoherence, that is, of inconsistencies and the mutual obstruction of various policies (as when adverse effects of EU agricultural subsidies on developing countries can be excluded). Stated "positively", policy coherence concerns the kind of policy interaction that strengthens development policy (as when migrants' remittances to their home countries contribute to development there) (Ashoff 2010b).[1] Coherence issues are also of vital importance at the level of international regimes (Kaul et al. 2003). The absence of regimes (as in the area of international migration policies) has effects on development policy, just as existing international regimes (in the form of international trade regimes, for example) do. In both cases, there can be development policy incoherence or positive, reinforcing effects.

6.2   Global public goods

The concept of public goods, which originates from economics, initially concerned the national level; since the late 1990s Inge Kaul and others have developed it into global public goods (GPG) approaches (Kaul et al. 2003; Kaul 2010; Severino / Ray 2009). Unlike private goods, public goods cannot be simply so arranged as to limit their benefit in an *excluding* and *exclusive* manner. Public goods are available to everyone, as in the form of security (for example, through the police) or public transport infrastructure (pavements, roads, traffic signs and so on). The increasingly cross-border nature of many aspects of life has led in recent years to an enormous surge of regionalisation and especially globalisation. Many public goods can no longer be made available at national level, or only to a very limited extent; this is true, for example, of security (we need think no further the phenomena of violence and crime) and of the protection and preservation of the natural environment (clean water). GPGs differ, for example, as regards the question whether people can be excluded from using them (excludability / non-excludability) or whether the use of a GPG is to the detriment of other users (rivalry / non-rivalry). Many GPGs are not made available in sufficient quantities, or they may be overused, one reason being that "free-riding" may be a rational model even for state action. The dual challenge in international cooperative relations – proliferation of actors and fragmented problem management – make the management of GPGs one of the most

DOI: 10.1057/9781137397881.0012

important tasks, necessitating, according to Severino und Ray (2010), new forms of collective action ("hypercollective action"). There is talk of multi-actor coalitions, which will facilitate communal action to the benefit of GPGs.

The provision of GPGs calls for cross-border action at regional or global level, including activities to curb or manage the consequences of climate change. For development cooperation an international approach geared to GPGs is relevant for two reasons. First, there is a growing need for policies and programmes in which states have a collective interest. Producing and financing these public goods is often difficult, but states too are susceptible to incentives not to participate in the provision of public goods (tragedy of the commons). Second, public goods made available in the context of development cooperation are typically not in the immediate interest of the supporting donors. Development aid has hitherto been largely geared to assisting a given country in its development process, without necessarily producing a global good. In the case of GPGs, on the other hand, the participating donors usually have a far greater self-interest; it may even be that such activities do not have a high priority for the country in which they are undertaken. It is therefore appropriate to make a distinction between activities for GPGs in the collective interest of all the participating actors and activities undertaken principally to the benefit of the development of the country in which they are promoted (Kaul 2013). There is a latent danger that aid is being used increasingly for the promotion of fundamentally new GPGs and so withheld from its original national development purposes.

Note

1   The Commitment to Development Index (CDI) published regularly by the Center for Global Development quantifies donor countries' efforts to make their development policies (and other contributions) coherent (http://www.cgdev.org/section/initiatives/active/cdi/).

DOI: 10.1057/9781137397881.0012

7
Development Cooperation: A Dinosaur?

Abstract: *From the outset, in the 1950s and 1960s, justifications for and conditions attached to development cooperation have changed continually. The changes in the 2000s in particular indicate that development policy is not only being constantly developed further and adapted, but is also undergoing fundamental reorientation. However, these reforms and changes are not always consistent and, indeed, often contradictory. On the one hand, the debate on aid effectiveness clearly reveals the call for development policy to be developed further and professionalised in respect of its core task of contributing to development processes in partner countries. On the other hand, the effectiveness agenda is lacking in its coverage of the reality of increasingly complex international cooperative relations.*

Klingebiel, Stephan. *Development Cooperation: Challenges of the New Aid Architecture.* Basingstoke: Palgrave Macmillan, 2014. DOI: 10.1057/9781137397881.0013.

From the outset, in the 1950s and 1960s, justifications for and conditions attached to development cooperation have changed continually. The changes in the 2000s in particular indicate that development policy is not only being constantly developed further and adapted, but is also undergoing fundamental reorientation. However, these reforms and changes are not always consistent and, indeed, often contradictory.

On the one hand, the debate on aid effectiveness clearly reveals the call for development policy to be developed further and professionalised in respect of its core task of contributing to development processes in partner countries. Nonetheless, at no time since its beginnings has development cooperation been free from tension or vested interests: indeed, it has often been dominated by the expediencies of foreign and foreign trade policy. The effectiveness debate and accompanying international negotiating processes have led to the systemic reform of development cooperation; the quality standards in development cooperation between the classical OECD donor world and the traditional recipient countries have been raised. Yet studies of individual donor practices and comparisons of donors show that it is far from easy to reform bi- and multilateral aid organisations. The rationality of donor actors tends very largely to promote proliferation, fragmentation and continuance. Moreover, conditions in partner countries for increasing aid effectiveness lack uniformity and are not, in some cases, conducive to development – as may be true of clientelistically organised countries.

On the other hand, the effectiveness agenda is lacking in its coverage of the reality of increasingly complex international cooperative relations. Various trends are to blame for this:

▶ First, the number of classical development cooperation partners is falling. There is a group of countries, especially in sub-Saharan Africa, that are still heavily dependent on aid, but, on the whole, the number of poor developing countries is on the decline. Development planning, management and allocation processes forming part of, say, poverty strategies will therefore wane in importance in the medium term.

▶ Second, the number of actors maintaining cooperative relations with developing countries has soared. They are the successful economies in the Asian region and cooperation partners from other of the world's regions (the Arab world and South America). The number of multilateral actors is also rising. Private actors (foundations and so on) too are gaining influence. In traditional development cooperation the competition has increased, while the influence wielded by the classical donors has decreased.

▸ Third, the aid instruments of the OECD donor world are no longer alone in setting international standards. Such donors as China and India do not feel in any way bound by the classical standard-setting function of the OECD's Development Assistance Committee. The instruments are therefore becoming more varied and, as regards the role of public and private or concessional and non-concessional resources, more complex.

▸ Fourth, there is, for all external actors, growing competition of interests between different globally aligned policy areas. This is true, for example, of international environment policy (climate financing) and security policy. The attempts traditionally made to keep development policy as free as possible from other interests and policies are being questioned by new global requirements.

An analysis of the current aid debate therefore entails far more than a look at technocratic aspects of development: it reveals the considerable need for development cooperation and other policies of relevance to developing countries to be redefined and reshaped to take account of new global challenges and new actors.

DOI: 10.1057/9781137397881.0013

Bibliography

Actionaid (2011) *Real aid: ending aid dependency* (London: Actionaid).

Adugna, A. et al. (2011) *Finance for development: trends and opportunities in a changing landscape*, CFP Working Paper No. 8 (Washington, DC: World Bank).

AfDB (African Development Bank) / OECD (Organisation for Economic Co-operation and Development) / UNDP (United Nations Development Programme) / UNECA (United Nations Economic Commission for Africa) (2012) *African economic outlook 2012* (Paris: OECD).

Altenburg, T. (2007) *From project to policy reform: experiences of German development cooperation*, Studies 27 (Bonn: Deutsches Institut für Entwicklungspolitik / German Development Institut (DIE)).

Altenburg, T. / A. Pegels (2012) 'Sustainability-oriented innovation systems: managing the green transformation', *Innovation and Development* 2 (1), Special Issue: Sustainability-oriented innovation systems in China and India, 5–22.

Andrews, M. (2013) *The limits of institutional reform in development: changing rules for realistic solutions* (New York: Cambridge University Press).

Ashoff, G. (2005) *Der entwicklungspolitische Kohärenzanspruch: Begründung, Anerkennung und Wege zu seiner Umsetzung*, Studies 6 (Bonn: Deutsches Institut für Entwicklungspolitik / German Development Institut (DIE)).

DOI: 10.1057/9781137397881.0014

_____ (2009) *Institutioneller Reformbedarf in der bilateralen staatlichen deutschen Entwicklungszusammenarbeit*, Analysen und Stellungnahmen 8 (Bonn: Deutsches Institut für Entwicklungspolitik / German Development Institut (DIE)).

_____ (2010a) 'Politikkohärenz: Eine zusätzliche Voraussetzung und wesentliche Aufgabe wirksamer Entwicklungspolitik' in J. Faust / S. Neubert (eds) *Wirksamere Entwicklungspolitik: Befunde, Reformen, Instrumente* (Baden-Baden: Nomos), 346–377.

_____ (2010b) 'Wirksamkeit als Legitimationsproblem und komplexe Herausforderung der Entwicklungspolitik' in J. Faust / S. Neubert (eds) *Wirksamere Entwicklungspolitik: Befunde, Reformen, Instrumente* (Baden-Baden: Nomos), 27–68.

Auswärtiges Amt / Bundesministerium der Verteidigung / Bundesministerium für wirtschaftliche Zusammenarbeit und Entwicklung (2012) *Für eine kohärente Politik der Bundesregierung gegenüber fragilen Staaten: Ressortübergreifende Leitlinien* (O.o.).

Banerjee, A. / E. Duflo (2011) *Poor economics: a radical rethinking of the way to fight global poverty* (New York: Public Affairs).

Barder, O. (2011) *Can aid work? Written testimony submitted to the House of Lords* (Washington, DC: Center for Global Development).

Besada, H. / S. Kindornay (eds) (2013) *Multilateral development cooperation in a changing global order* (Basingstoke: Palgrave Macmillan).

Bigsten, A. L. / J. P. Platteau / S. Tengstam (2011) *The aid effectiveness agenda: the benefits of going ahead* (Brussels: EU).

Birdsall, N. (2011) 'The global financial crisis: the beginning of the end of the "development" agenda?' in N. Birdsall / F. Fukuyama (eds) *New ideas on development after the financial crisis* (Baltimore: John Hopkins University Press), 1–26.

Birdsall, N. / H. Kharas (2010) *Quality of official development assistance assessment* (Washington, DC: Brookings Institution and Centre for Global Development).

Birdsall, N. / H. Kharas / R. Perakis (2012) *The quality of official development assistance assessment 2009: is aid quality improving?* (Washington, DC: Brookings Institution and Center for Global Development).

Birdsall, N. / W. D. Savedoff (2010) *Cash on delivery: a new approach to foreign aid* (Washington, DC: Center for Global Development).

DOI: 10.1057/9781137397881.0014

BMZ (Bundesministerium für wirtschaftliche Zusammenarbeit und Entwicklung) (2011) *Deutsche Entwicklungspolitik auf einen Blick* (Paderborn / Köln).

_____ (ed.) (2012) *Auf Augenhöhe, 50 Jahre Bundesministerium für wirtschaftliche Zusammenarbeit und Entwicklung* (Baden-Baden: Nomos).

_____ (2013) *Geber im Vergleich 2012 – Veränderung gegenüber 2011*, http://www.bmz.de/de/ministerium/zahlen_fakten/Geber_im_Vergleich-Veraenderung_2012_gegenueber_2011.pdf, date accessed 02 March 2013.

Boone, P. (1996) 'Politics and the effectiveness of foreign aid', *European Economic Review* 40, 289–329.

Braeutigam, D. (2009) *The dragon's gift: the real story of China in Africa* (Oxford: Oxford University Press).

Braeutigam, D. / S. Knack (2004) 'Foreign aid, institutions, and governance in sub-saharan Africa', *Economic Development and Cultural Change* 52 (2), 255–285.

Brock, L. / N. Deitelhoff (2012) 'Der normative Bezugsrahmen der internationalen Politik: Schutzverantwortung und Friedenspflicht' in B. Schoch et al. (eds) *Friedensgutachten 2012* (Berlin: LIT Verlag), 99–111.

Buchner, B. et al. (2011) *The landscape of climate finance*, CPI Report (Venedig: Climate Policy Initiative).

Burnside, C. / D. Dollar (2000) 'Aid, policies, and growth', *The American Economic Review* 90, 847–868.

Chaturvedi, S. / T. Fues / E. H. Sidiropoulos (eds) (2012) *Development cooperation and emerging powers. New partners or old patterns?* (London / New York: Zed Books).

Chen, S. / M. Ravallion (2012) *An update to the World Bank's estimates of consumption poverty in the developing world*, World Bank Briefing Note (Washington, DC: World Bank).

Clay, E. J. / M. Geddes / L. Natali (2009) *Untying aid: is it working? An evaluation of the implementationof the Paris Declaration and of the 2001 DAC recommendation of untying ODA to the LDCs* (Copenhagen: Danish Institute for International Studies).

Collier, P. (2006a) *Assisting Africa to achieve decisive change* (Oxford: Centre for the Study of African Economies).

_____ (2006b) 'Is aid oil? An analysis of whether Africa can absorb more aid', *World Development* 34, 1482–1497.

DOI: 10.1057/9781137397881.0014

____ (2008) *The bottom billion. Why the poorest countries are failing and what can be done about it* (Oxford: Oxford University Press).

Daase, C. (2010) 'Wandel der Sicherheitskultur', *Aus Politik und Zeitgeschichte* 50, 9–16.

Davies, P. (2011) 'Toward a new development cooperation dynamic' in North-South Institute (ed.) *Canadian development report 2011: global challenges: multilateral solutions* (Ottawa: The North-South Institute), 79–93.

Debiel, T. / N. Goede (2011) 'Militärinterventionen und Stabilisierungseinsätze: eine kritische Zwischenbilanz' in M. Johannsen et al. (eds) *Friedensgutachten 2011* (Berlin: LIT Verlag), 194–207.

DFID (Department for International Development) (2011) *Multilateral aid review* (London: DFID).

____ (2012) *Annual report and account 2011–2012* (London: DFID).

de Renzio, P. (2006) *Promoting mutual accountability in aid relationships*, Briefing Paper 1 (London: Overseas Development Institute).

Easterly, W. (2002) 'The cartel of good intentions: the problem of bureaucracy in foreign aid', *Journal of Policy Reform* 5 (4), 1–28.

____ (2003) 'Can foreign aid buy growth?', *Journal of Economic Perspectives* 3 (17), 23–48.

____ (2006) *The white man's burden: why the West's efforts to aid the rest have done so much ill and so little good* (Oxford / New York: Oxford University Press, Frankfurt a. M.: Campus).

____ (2008): *Reinventing foreign aid* (Cambridge, MA: The MIT Press).

European Report on Development (ERD) (2013) *Post 2015: global action for an inclusive and sustainable future* (Brussels: Overseas Development Institute (ODI) / Deutsches Institut für Entwicklungspolitik / German Development Institute (DIE) / European Centre for Development Policy Management (ECDPM)).

Faust, J. / S. Leiderer (2008) 'Zur Effektivität und politischen Ökonomie in der Entwicklungszusammenarbeit', *Politische Vierteljahresschrift* 49 (1), 129–152.

____ (2010) 'Die Effektivität der Entwicklungszusammenarbeit: Ergebnisse des ökonometrischen Ländervergleichs' in J. Faust / S. Neubert (eds) *Wirksamere Entwicklungspolitik: Befunde, Reformen, Instrumente* (Baden-Baden: Nomos), 166–188.

DOI: 10.1057/9781137397881.0014

Faust, J. / S. Neubert (eds) (2010) *Wirksamere Entwicklungspolitik: Befunde, Reformen, Instrumente* (Baden-Baden: Nomos).

Fues, T. / S. Klingebiel (2007) 'Multilaterale Entwicklungszusammenarbeit: die Rolle der Vereinten Nationen' in H. Volger (eds) *Grundlagen und Strukturen der Vereinten Nationen* (München: Oldenbourg Verlag), 219–241.

Fues, T. (2010) 'Zur Wirksamkeit der Entwicklungszusammenarbeit der Vereinten Nationen' in J. Faust / S. Neubert (eds) *Wirksamere Entwicklungspolitik: Befunde, Reformen, Instrumente* (Baden-Baden: Nomos), 403–430.

Fues, T. / P. Wolff (eds) (2010) *G20 and global development: how can the new summit architecture promote pro-poor growth and sustainability?* (Bonn: Deutsches Institut für Entwicklungspolitik / German Development Institute (DIE)).

Fues, T. / Y. Liu (eds) (2011) *Global governance and building a harmonious world: a comparison of European and Chinese concepts for international affairs,* Studies 62 (Bonn: Deutsches Institut für Entwicklungspolitik / German Development Institute (DIE), in cooperation with China Institute of International Studies (CIIS)).

Furness, M. (2012a) 'The Lisbon treaty, the European external action service and the reshaping of EU development policy' in S. Grimm / D. Makhan / S. Gänzle (eds) *The European Union and global development: an 'enlightened superpower' in the making?* (Basingstoke: Palgrave Macmillan), 74–93.

_____ (2012b) 'African-European relations' in A. Mehler / H. Melber / K. van Walraven (eds) *Africa yearbook: politics, economy and society south of the Sahara in 2011* (Leiden: Brill), 29–43.

Furness, M. / I. Scholz / A. Guarín (2012) *History repeats? The rise of the new middle classes in the developing world*, Briefing Paper 19 (Bonn: Deutsches Institut für Entwicklungspolitik / German Development Institute (DIE)).

Gänzle, S. / B. Franke (2010) 'Afrikanische Friedens- und Sicherheitsarchitektur: Institutionalisierte Zusammenarbeit in und für Afrika', *Aus Politik und Zeitgeschichte* 50, 31–37.

Gänzle, S. / S. Grimm / D. Makhan (eds) (2012) *The European Union and global development: an 'enlightened superpower' in the making?* (Basingstoke: Palgrave Macmillan).

Gibson, C. C. et al. (2005) *The Samaritan's dilemma: the political economy of development aid* (Oxford: Oxford University Press).

DOI: 10.1057/9781137397881.0014

Grävingholt, J. / C. Hofmann / S. Klingebiel (2007) *Development cooperation and non-state armed groups*, Studies 29 (Bonn: Deutsches Institut für Entwicklungspolitik / German Development Institute (DIE)).

Grävingholt, J. / J. Leininger / O. Schlumberger (2009) 'Demokratieförderung: Quo Vadis?', *Aus Politik und Zeitgeschichte* 8, 28–33.

Grävingholt, J. / J. Leininger / C. von Haldenwang (2012) *Effective statebuilding? A review of evaluations of international statebuilding support in fragile contexts*, Evaluation Study 3 (Copenhagen: Ministry of Foreign Affairs of Denmark (DANIDA)).

Greig, A. / D. Hulme / M. Turner (2007) *Challenging global inequality: development theory and practice in the 21st century* (New York: Palgrave).

Grimm, S. (2010) 'Zur Wirksamkeit der europäischen Entwicklungspolitik' in J. Faust / S. Neubert (eds) (2010) *Wirksamere Entwicklungspolitik: Befunde, Reformen, Instrumente* (Baden-Baden: Nomos), 381–402.

Grimm, S. / C. Hackenesch (2012) 'European engagement with emerging actors in development: forging new partnerships?' in S. Gänzle / S. Grimm / D. Makhan (eds) *The European Union and global development: an 'enlightened superpower' in the making?* (Basingstoke: Palgrave Macmillan), 211–228.

Grimm, S. / D. Makhan / S. Gänzle (eds) (2012) *The European Union and global development: an 'enlightened superpower' in the making?* (Basingstoke: Palgrave Macmillan).

Grittner, A. M. (2013) *Results-based financing: evidence from performance-based financing in the health sector*, Discussion Paper 06 (Bonn: German Development Institute / Deutsches Institut für Entwicklungspolitik (DIE)).

Hackenesch, C. (2009) *China and the EU's engagement in Africa: setting the stage for cooperation, competition or conflict?*, Discussion Paper 16 (Bonn: Deutsches Institut für Entwicklungspolitik / German Development Institute (DIE)).

Harris, D. / M. Moore / H. Schmitz (2009) *Country classifications for a changing world*, Discussion Paper 9 (Bonn: Deutsches Institut für Entwicklungspolitik / German Development Institut (DIE)).

Haslam, P. A. / J. Schafer / P. Beaudet (2012) *Introduction to international development: approaches, actors, and issues*, 2nd edition (Ontario: Oxford University Press).

DOI: 10.1057/9781137397881.0014

Heller, P. S. (2011) *Rethinking the world of aid in the twenty first century* (Helsinki: UNU-WIDER).

Hoeffler, A. (2012) *Growth, aid and policies in countries recovering from war: a thematic paper supporting OECD DAC INCAF project 'Global Factors Influencing the Risk of Conflict and Fragility'* (Paris: OECD).

Ihne, H. / J. H. Wilhelm (eds) (2006) *Einführung in die Entwicklungspolitik* (Münster: LIT Verlag).

Ihne, H. / J. H. Wilhelm (2006) 'Grundlagen der Entwicklungspolitik' in H. Ihne / J. H. Wilhelm (eds) *Einführung in die Entwicklungspolitik* (Münster: LIT Verlag), 1–40.

IMF (International Monetary Fund) (2012) *Sub-Saharan Africa: maintaining growth in an uncertain world,* Regional Economic Outlook (Washington, DC: IMF).

Janus, H. (2012) *External support to national development efforts, literature* review (draft) (Bonn: Deutsches Institut für Entwicklungspolitik / German Development Institut (DIE)).

Janus, H. / S. Klingebiel (2012) *Die Post-2015 Entwicklungsagenda: Erster Spatenstich für eine neue globale Entwicklungsagenda,* Kolumne vom 10.09.2012 (Bonn: Deutsches Institut für Entwicklungspolitik / German Development Institut (DIE)).

Jerven, M. (2013) *Poor numbers: how we are misled by african development statistics and what to do about it* (Ithaca / London: Cornell University Press).

Karns, M. P. / K. A. Mingst (2010) *International organizations: the politics and processes of global governance* (Boulder / London: Lynne Rienner Publishers).

Kaul, I. (2010) 'Souveränität wiedergewinnen: Suche nach den Grundelementen eines neuen Multilateralismus', *Aus Politik und Zeitgeschichte* 34–35, 34–40.

_____ (2013) *Global Public Goods: a concept for framing the post-2015 agenda?,* Discussion Paper 2 (Bonn: Deutsches Institut für Entwicklungspolitik / German Development Institut (DIE)).

Kaul, I. et al. (2003) *Providing global public goods: managing globalization* (New York / Oxford: Oxford University Press).

Keely, B. (2012) *From aid to development: the global fight against poverty,* OECD Insights, OECD Publishing; http://www.oecd-ilibrary.org/docserver/download/0111101e.pdf?expires=1368693106&id=id&accname=guest&checksum=91DC6512D1C710B3C8A3792177DCD28D, date accessed 07 January 2013.

DOI: 10.1057/9781137397881.0014

Keohane, R. O. / S. Macedo / A. Moravcsik (2009) 'Democracy-enhancing multilateralism', *International Organizations* 63, Winter 2009, 1–31.

Kharas, H. (2012) *Global partnership for effective development cooperation* (Washington, DC: The Brookings Institution). (Policy Paper 2012–04)

Kharas, H. / K. Makino / W. Jung (2011) 'Overview: an agenda for the Busan high-level forum on aid effectiveness' in H. Kharas / K. Makino / W. Jung (eds) *Catalyzing development: a new vision for aid* (Washington, DC: Brookings Institution Press), 1–37.

Klingebiel, S. (1993) 'Multilaterale Entwicklungspolitik', *Aus Politik und Zeitgeschichte, Beilage zur Wochenzeitung Das Parlament*, Nr. B 12–13, 19. März 1993.

_____ (2003) *Der internationale Diskussionsstand über Programmorientierung: Schlussfolgerungen für die internationale und deutsche Entwicklungszusammenarbeit*, Berichte und Gutachten 5 (Bonn: Deutsches Institut für Entwicklungspolitik / German Development Institut (DIE)).

_____ (2005) *How much aid is good for Africa – a big push as a way out of the "poverty trap"?*,Briefing Paper 4 (Bonn: Deutsches Institut für Entwicklungspolitik / German Development Institut (DIE)).

_____ (2006a) *Mehr Geld – mehr Wirkung? Neue Risiken durch vermehrte Entwicklungshilfe*, Focus Nr. 11 (Hamburg: GIGA (German Institut of Global and Area Studies)).

_____ (2006b) 'Converging the role of development policy and security policy? New approaches in Africa' in Klingebiel (eds) *New interfaces between security and development: changing concepts and approaches*, Study 13 (Bonn: Deutsches Institut für Entwicklungspolitik / German Development Institut (DIE)), 127–145.

_____ (2010) 'Wirksamkeit und Absorptionsfähigkeit der Partnerländer' in J. Faust / S. Neubert (eds) (2010) *Wirksamere Entwicklungspolitik: Befunde, Reformen, Instrumente* (Baden-Baden: Nomos), 289–304

_____ (2011a) *Ergebnisbasierte Entwicklungszusammenarbeit: Grenzen neuer Ansätze*, Analysen und Stellungnahmen 15 (Bonn: Deutsches Institut für Entwicklungspolitik / German Development Institut (DIE)).

_____ (2011b) *Stellungnahme zum Thema "Budgethilfen"*, Schriftliche Stellungnahme im Rahmen der öffentlichen Anhörung des Deutschen Bundestages (Kigali: Ausschuss für wirtschaftliche Zusammenarbeit und Entwicklung).

DOI: 10.1057/9781137397881.0014

_____ (2012a) *Stellungnahme zur Öffentlichen Anhörung des Ausschusses für wirtschaftliche Zusammenarbeit und Entwicklung zum Thema "Bilaterale und multilaterale Entwicklungszusammenarbeit"* (Bonn: Deutsches Institut für Entwicklungspolitik / German Development Institut (DIE)).

_____ (2012b) *Entwicklungszusammenarbeit: Auslaufmodell oder Entwicklungsmotor für Subsahara-Afrika?*, Analysen und Stellungnahmen 3 (Bonn: Deutsches Institut für Entwicklungspolitik / German Development Institut (DIE)).

_____ (2012c) *Results-Based Aid (RBA): new aid approaches, limitations and the application to promote good governance*, Discussion Paper 14 (Bonn: Deutsches Institut für Entwicklungspolitik / German Development Institut (DIE)).

Klingebiel, S. (ed.) (2006) *New interfaces between security and development: changing concepts and approaches*, Study 13 (Bonn: Deutsches Institut für Entwicklungspolitik / German Development Institut (DIE)).

Klingebiel, S. / S. Leiderer (2011) *Aid effectiveness der zwei Geschwindigkeiten*, Kolumne vom 05.12.2011 (Bonn: Deutsches Institut für Entwicklungspolitik / German Development Institut (DIE)).

Klingebiel, S. / S. Leiderer / P. Schmidt (2007) *Wie wirksam sind neue Modalitäten der Entwicklungszusammenarbeit? Erste Erfahrungen mit Programme-Based Approaches (PBA)*, Discussion Paper 7 (Bonn: Deutsches Institut für Entwicklungspolitik / German Development Institut (DIE)).

:Klingebiel, S. / K. Roehder (2008) 'Interfaces between development and security: converging the role of development policy and security policy?' in H. G. Brauch et al. (eds) *Globalisation and environmental challenges: reconceptualising security in the 21st century* (Berlin [u.a.]: Springer), 743–752.

Klingebiel, S. et al. (2008) *Donor contributions to strengthening the African peace and security architecture*, Studies 38 (Bonn: Deutsches Institut für Entwicklungspolitik / German Development Institut (DIE)).

Klingebiel, S. / T. Mahn (2011) *Die Reform der öffentlichen Finanzsysteme in Entwicklungsländern als Beitrag zur Verbesserung der Regierungsführung*, Analysen und Stellungnahmen 5/2011(Bonn: Deutsches Institut für Entwicklungspolitik / German Development Institut (DIE)).

DOI: 10.1057/9781137397881.0014

Klingebiel, S. / T. C. Mahn (2013) 'Strenghtening the accountability of local governance: how to bridge the gap between decentralisation and public finance management', The Broker, http://www.thebrokeronline.eu/Articles/Strenghtening-the-accountability-of-local-governance, date accessed 29 March 2013.

Koch, S. (2012) *From poverty reduction to mutual interests? The debate on differentiation in EU development policy*, Discussion Paper 13 (Bonn: Deutsches Institut für Entwicklungspolitik / German Development Institut (DIE)).

Leiderer, S. (2012a) *Fungibility and the choice of aid modalities: the red herring revisited* (Helsinki: UNU-Wider).

____ (2012b): 'Wirksamere Entwicklungszusammenarbeit durch Budgethilfe? Theorie und Praxis eines umstrittenen Instruments' in R. Öhlschläger / H. Sangmeister (eds) *Neue Formen und Instrumente der Entwicklungszusammenarbeit* (Baden-Baden: Nomos), 97–110.

Liebig, K. / G. Ressel / U. Rondorf (2008) *Dutch disease: Ökonomische Prozesse und Implikationen für die Entwicklungszusammenarbeit*, Discussion Paper 21 (Bonn: Deutsches Institut für Entwicklungspolitik / German Development Institut (DIE)).

Loewe, M. (2012) *Nach 2015: wie lassen sich die Millennium Development Goals mit den in Rio beschlossenen Sustainable Development Goals verbinden?*, Analysen und Stellungnahmen 14 (Bonn: Deutsches Institut für Entwicklungspolitik / German Development Institut (DIE)).

Loewe, M. / N. Ripping (2012) *Globale Armutsstrukturen im Wandel*, Analysen und Stellungnahmen 7 (Bonn: Deutsches Institut für Entwicklungspolitik / German Development Institut (DIE)).

Lundsgaarde, E. (2010) *Emerging non-state actors in global development: challenges for Europe* (Bonn: EADI).

____ (2013) *Complementarity in development: bringing private foundations on board*, Briefing Paper 10 (Bonn: Deutsches Institut für Entwicklungspolitik / German Development Institut (DIE)).

Lundsgaarde, E. (ed.) (2012) *Africa toward 2030, challenges for development policy* (Basingstoke: Palgrave Macmillan).

Lundsgaarde, E. / M. Roch (2012) 'Mapping development trends in Africa' in Lundsgaarde (ed.) (2012) *Africa toward 2030: challenges for development policy* (Basingstoke: Palgrave Macmillan), 36–62.

Mahn, T. (2012) *The financing of development cooperation at the United Nations: why more means less*, Briefing Paper 8 (Bonn: Deutsches

DOI: 10.1057/9781137397881.0014

Institut für Entwicklungspolitik / German Development Institut (DIE)).

Manning, R. (2012) *Aid as a Second-Best Solution: Seven Problems of Effectiveness and How to Tackle Them*, Working Paper No 2012/24, Helsinki: UNU-Wider.

Mallet, R. / A. Sumner (2013) *The future of foreign aid: development cooperation and the new geography of global poverty* (Basingstoke: Palgrave Macmillan).

Maxwell, S. / D. Messner (2011) 'Fokus auf globale Entwicklung', *E+Z Entwicklung und Zusammenarbeit* 52 (10), 379–381.

McGillivray, M. et al. (2006) 'Controversies over the impact of development aid: it works; it doesn't; it can, but that depends', *Journal of International Development* 18, 1031–1050.

MDG Monitor (s.a.) *Tracking the Millennium Development Goals: browse by goal, an initiative of the United Nations*; http://www.mdgmonitor. org/browse_goal.cfm, date accessed 18 April 2013.

Menzel, U. (1992) *Das Ende der Dritten Welt und das Scheitern der großen Theorie* (Frankfurt am Main: Suhrkamp).

Messner, D. / F. Nuscheler (2003) *Das Konzept Global Governance. Stand und Perspektiven*, INEF-Report 67 (Duisburg: Institut für Entwicklung und Frieden (INEF) der Universität Duisburg-Essen).

Messner, D. / I. Scholz (eds) (2005) *Zukunftsfragen der Entwicklungspolitik* (Baden-Baden: Nomos).

Messner, D. / R. Kaplinksy (eds) (2008) 'The impact of Asian drivers on the developing world', *World Development* 36 (2), 197–209.

Messner, D. / J. Faust (2012) 'Probleme globaler Entwicklung und die ministerielle Organisation der Entwicklungspolitik', *Zeitschrift für Außen- und Sicherheitspolitik* 2 (5), 165–176.

Milner, H. V. / D. Tingley (2012) 'The choice of multilateralism: foreign aid and American foreign policy', *The Review of International Organizations* 6 (3–4), 313–341.

Moss, T. et al. (2006) *An aid-institutions paradox? A review essay on aid dependency and state building in sub-Saharan Africa*, Working Paper No. 74 (Washington, DC: Center for Global Development).

Moss, T. / G. Pettersson / N. van de Walle (2008) 'An aid-institutions paradox? A review essay on aid dependency and state building in sub-Saharan Africa' in W. Easterly (ed.) *Reinventing foreign aid* (Cambridge, MA: The MIT Press), 255–281.

DOI: 10.1057/9781137397881.0014

Moyo, D. (2009) *Dead aid: why aid is not working and how there is another way for Africa* (London: Allan Lane).

Nohlen, D. / F. Nuscheler (1982) 'Was heißt Entwicklung?' in D. Nohlen / F. Nuscheler (eds) *Handbuch der Dritten Welt. Unterentwicklung und Entwicklung: Theorien, Strategien, Indikatoren*, Band 1 (Hamburg: Hoffmann und Campe), 11–24.

North-South Institute (eds) (2011) *Canadian development report 2011: global challenges: multilateral solutions* (Ottawa: The North-South Institute).

Nuscheler, F. (2006) *Entwicklungspolitik* (Bonn: Bundeszentrale für politische Bildung).

ODI (Overseas Development Institute), DIE (Deutsches Institut für Entwicklungspolitik), FRIDE (Fundación para las Relaciones Internacionales y el Diálogo Exterior) / ECDPM (European Centre for Development Policy Management) (eds) (2010) *New challenges, new beginnings: next steps in European development cooperation* (London: European Think-Tanks Group).

OECD (Organisation for Economic Co-operation and Development) (2010) *Perspectives on global development 2010: shifting wealth* (Paris: OECD).

_____ (2011a) *Perspectives on global development 2012: social cohesion in a shifting world* (Paris: OECD).

_____ (2011b) *Aid effectiveness 2005–10: progress in implementing the Paris Declaration* (OECD Publishing).

_____ (s.a.) *DAC lists of ODA recipients: effective for reporting on 2012 and 2013 flows,* http://www.oecd.org/dac/stats/DAC%20List%20used%20for%202012%20and%202013%20flows.pdf, date accessed 05 April 2013.

OECD (Organisation for Economic Co-operation and Development)/ DAC (Development Assistance Committee) (2010a) *Deutschland: peer review 2010* (Paris: OECD).

_____ (2010b) *Development cooperation report 2010* (Paris: OECD).

_____ (2011a) *DAC report on multilateral aid* (Paris: OECD).

_____ (2011b) *Development cooperation report 2011: 50th anniversary edition* (Paris: OECD).

_____ (2011c) *2011 OECD report on division of labour: addressing cross-country fragmentation of aid* (Paris: OECD).

_____ (2012a) *Development cooperation report 2012* (Paris: OECD).

DOI: 10.1057/9781137397881.0014

_____ (2012b) *The architecture of development assistance*, OECD Publishing http://www.oecd-ilibrary.org/development/the-architecture-of-development-assistance-2012_9789264178885-en, date accessed 11 December 2012.

_____ (2012c) *Fragile States 2013: resource flows and trends in a shifting world*, DAC International Network on Conflict and Fragility (Paris: OECD).

_____ (2013a) *2012 DAC report on multilateral aid*, draft: 07 February 2013 (Paris: OECD).

_____ (2013b) *Country Programmable Aid: DAC countries*, http://webnet.oecd.org/dcdgraphs/CPA_donor/, date accessed 14 March 2013.

_____ (2013c) *Getting closer to the core: measuring country programmable aid*, http://www.oecd.org/dac/stats/gettingclosertothecore-measuringcountryprogrammableaid.htm, date accessed 13 March 2013.

Öhlschläger, R. / H. Sangmeister (eds) (2012) *Neue Formen und Instrumente der Entwicklungszusammenarbeit* (Baden-Baden: Nomos).

Orbie, J. (2012) 'The EU's role in development: a full-fledged development actor or eclipsed by superpower temptations?' in S. Gänzle / S. Grimm / D. Makhan (eds) *The European Union and global development: an 'enlightened superpower' in the making?* (Basingstoke: Palgrave Macmillan), 17–13.

Ostrom, E. et al. (2002) 'Aid, incentives, and sustainability: an institutional analysis of development cooperation', *Sida Studies in Evaluation* (Stockholm: SIDA (Swedish International Development Authority)).

Ottaway, M. (2007) 'Entwicklungszusammenarbeit in fragile Staaten' in Bundesministerium für wirtschaftliche Zusammenarbeit und Entwicklung (eds) (2007) *Fragile Staaten: Beispiele aus der entwicklungspolitischen Praxis* (Baden-Baden: Nomos), 11–20.

Parliament UK (2012) *EU Aid instruments and organizations*, http://www.publications.parliament.uk/pa/cm201012/cmselect/cmintdev/1680/168005.htm, date accessed 13 March 2013.

Paulo, S. / H. Reisen (2011) 'China, Indien, Afrika: den Entwicklungsdialog neu definieren' in J. M. Nebe (eds) *Herausforderung Afrika: Gesellschaft und Raum im Wandel* (Baden-Baden: Nomos Verl.-Ges.), 411–418.

Pereira J. / C. Villota (2012) *Hitting the target? Evaluating the effectiveness of results-based approaches to aid* (Brussels: Eurodad).

DOI: 10.1057/9781137397881.0014

Picciotto, R. (2011) 'Multilateral development cooperation and the Paris process: the road to Busan' in North-South Institute (eds) *Canadian Development Report 2011: global challenges: multilateral solutions* (Ottawa), 55–76.

Radelet, S. (2006) *A primer on foreign aid*, Working Paper 92 (Washington, DC: Center for Global Development).

____ (2010) *Emerging Africa: how 17 countries are leading the way* (Washington, DC: Center for Global Development).

Rauch, T. (2009) *Entwicklungspolitik* (Braunschweig: Westermann).

Reisen, H. (2009) 'The multilateral donor non-system: towards accountability and efficient role assignment', *Economics, The Open-Access, Open-Assessment E-Journal* (2009–2018), Special Issue Global Governance – Challenges and Proposals for Reform.

Rietjens, S. / M. Bollen (eds) (2008) *Managing civil-military cooperation: a 24/7 joint effort for stability* (Aldershot / Burlington: Ashgate).

Rodrik, D. (2011) *The globalization paradox: democracy and the future of the world economy* (New York: W. W. Norton & Company).

Rodrik, D. / M. R. Rosenzweig (2010) *Handbook of development economics* (Amsterdam i.a.: Elsevier).

Rogerson, A. (2011) *What if development aid were truly 'catalytic'?* Background note (London: Overseas Development Institute).

Sachs, J. (2005) *The end of poverty. How we can make it happen in our lifetime* (London: Penguin).

Sangmeister, H. / A. Schönstedt (2010) *Entwicklungszusammenarbeit im 21. Jahrhundert* (Baden-Baden: Nomos).

Schellnhuber, H. J. / D. Messner et al. (2011) *World in transition: a social contract for sustainability,* Flagship Report (Berlin: German Advisory Council on Global Change (WBGU)).

Scholz, I. (2010) 'Wandel durch Klimawandel? Wachstum und ökologische Grenzen in Brasilien', *Aus Parlament und Zeitgeschichte* 12, 22–28.

Severino, J.-M. / O. Ray (2009) *The end of ODA: death and rebirth of a global public policy* (Washington, DC: Center for Global Development).

____ (2010): *The end of ODA (II): the birth of hypercollective action,* Working Paper (Washington, DC: Center for Global Development).

Shaohua, C. / M. Ravallion (2012) *The landscape of climate finance. A CPI report* (Washington, DC: World Bank).

DOI: 10.1057/9781137397881.0014

Spence, M. (2011) *The next convergence: the future of economic growth in a multispeed world* (New York: Farrar, Straus and Giroux).

Stamm, A. (2004) *Schwellen- und Ankerländer als Akteure einer globalen Partnerschaft, Überlegungen zu einer Positionsbestimmung aus deutscher entwicklungspolitischer Sicht*, Discussion Paper 1 (Bonn: Deutsches Institut für Entwicklungspolitik / German Development Institute (DIE)).

Stockmann, R. / U. Menzel / F. Nuscheler (2010) *Entwicklungspolitik. Theorien, Probleme, Strategien* (München: Oldenbourg).

Sumner, A. (2010) *Global poverty and the new bottom billion: what if three-quarters of the world's poor live in middle-income countries?*, Working Paper (Sussex: Institute for Development Studies).

_____ (2012): 'Where do the poor live?', *World Development* 40 (5), 865–877.

Temple, J. (2010) 'Aid and conditionality' in D. Rodrik / M. R. Rosenzweig (eds) (2010) *Handbook of development economics* (Amsterdam i.a.: Elsevier), 4415–4523.

_____ (2012) 'Where do the poor live?', *World Development* 40, 865–877.

UN (United Nations) (2011a) *Millenniums-Entwicklungsziele, Bericht 2011* (New York: UN).

_____ (2011b) *Programme of action for the least developed countries for the decade 2011–2020* (New York: UN).

UNCTAD (United Nations Conference on Trade and Development) (2011) *The least developed countries report 2011: the potential role of south-south cooperation for inclusive and sustainable development* (New York / Genf: UNCTAD).

UNDESA (Department of Economic and Social Affairs) (2010) *International Development Cooperation Report: Development cooperation for the MDGs: maximising results*, UN Document. ST/ESA/326 (New York: UN).

Vollmer, F. (2012) *Increasing the visibility and effectiveness of development cooperation: how to reconcile two competing objectives?*, Study 67 (Bonn: Deutsches Institut für Entwicklungspolitik / German Development Institut (DIE)).

Volz, U. (2012) *The need and scope for strengthening co-operation between regional financing arrangements and the IMF*, Discussion Paper 15 (Bonn: Deutsches Institut für Entwicklungspolitik / German Development Institut (DIE)).

DOI: 10.1057/9781137397881.0014

Walz, J. / V. Ramachandran (2011) *Brave new world, a literature review of emerging donors and the changing nature of foreign assistance* (Washington, DC: Center for Global Development).

WBGU (Wissenschaftlicher Beirat der Bundesregierung Globale Umweltveränderungen) (2011) *Welt im Wandel: Gesellschaftsvertrag für eine Große Transformation* (Berlin: WBGU).

Weinlich, S. (2010) *Die Reform der Entwicklungszusammenarbeit der Vereinten Nationen*, Studies 55 (Bonn: Deutsches Institut für Entwicklungspolitik / German Development Institut (DIE)).

_____ (2012) 'Die Entwicklungszusammenarbeit der Vereinten Nationen: Reformbedarf und aktuelle Reformansätze' in R. Öhlschläger / H. Sangmeister (eds) *Neue Formen der Entwicklungszusammenarbeit* (Baden-Baden: Nomos), 157–170.

Weinlich, S. / S. Grimm (2009) *Die Entwicklungszusammenarbeit der EU und der UN: Wofür sollte sich Deutschland einsetzen?*, *Analysen und Stellungnahmen*, 13 (Bonn: Deutsches Institut für Entwicklungspolitik / German Development Institut (DIE)).

Wolff, J. H. (2005) *Entwicklungshilfe: Ein hilfreiches Gewerbe?* (Berlin: LIT Verlag).

Wolff, P. (2011) 'Auswirkungen der Finanzkrise auf die Entwicklungsländer: Handlungsoptionen für die Entwicklungspolitik' in G. Meyer / A. Thimm (eds) *Wirtschaftliche und soziale Folgen der Finanzkrise für die Entwicklungsländer*, Veröffentlichungen des interdisziplinären Arbeitskreises Dritte Welt 21 (Mainz: Johannes Gutenberg Univ.), 9–18.

Wood, B. et al. (2011) *The evaluation of the Paris Declaration, Phase 2, Final Report* (Aarhus: Danish Institute for International Studies).

World Bank (2005) *Remittances: development impact and future prospects* (Washington, DC: World Bank).

_____ (2011a) *World development report 2011: conflict, security, and development* (Washington, DC: World Bank).

_____ (2011b) *Finance and opportunities in a changing landscape*, CFP Working Paper No. 8. (Washington, DC.).

World Bank / IFC (International Finance Cooperation) (2012) *Doing business 2013* (Washington, DC: World Bank / IFC).

Zimmermann, F. / K. Smith (2011) 'More actors, more money, more ideas for international development co-operation', *Journal of International Development* 23, 722–738.

DOI: 10.1057/9781137397881.0014

Additional links

Platform 'New Deal Building Peaceful States' (English) http://www.
newdeal4peace.org/

Für eine kohärente Politik der Bundesregierung gegenüber fragilen
Staaten – Ressortübergreifende Leitlinien (German) http://
www.auswaertiges-amt.de/cae/servlet/contentblob/626516/
publicationFile/171903/120919_Leitlinien_Fragile_Staaten.pdf

OECD-Directorate for development cooperation (DCD-DAC) (English)
http://www.oecd.org/dac

VN Millennium Development Goals (German) http://www.unric.org/
html/german/mdg/index.html

World Bank (English) http://www.worldbank.org

Deutsches Institut für Entwicklungspolitik / German Development
Institute (German / English) http://www.die-gdi.de

Friedensgutachten / Peace report (German / English) http://www.
friedensgutachten.de/index.php/id-2012.html

DOI: 10.1057/9781137397881.0014

Index

accountability, 76–80
Accra Agenda for Action, 72
Afghanistan, 7, 10, 42, 45
African Development
    Bank, 25
African Union, 44, 47
aid concentration ratio, 32
aid effectiveness, 27–9,
    66–85, 92
aid modalities, 57
aid orphans, 27
aid to GNI ratio, 7
altruism, 11
Angola, 20, 42, 48
Arab donors, 19, 70
Asia, 5, 92
asylum, 10–11
Australia, 24

Belgium, 10
beyond aid, 87–9
bilateral aid / development
    cooperation, 20–6, 31–3
Bill and Melinda Gates
    Foundation (BMGF),
    20, 73
Botswana, 49
Brazil, 16, 19–20, 37, 73
budget support, 58–9
Burundi, 7, 42, 49
Busan summit, 72–4
business community, 10

Canada, 24
CARE, 20

Cash on Delivery approach,
    62–3
Centre for Global
    Development (CGD), 60
Chile, 19–20
China, 16, 19–20, 37, 38, 68, 70,
    72, 73
churches, 11
civil society, 11
climate change, 11
Cold War, 9–10
colonies, 10
Commitment to Development
    Index (CDI), 90n1
complementarity, 26
concessional loans, 3
conflict management, 41–7
country classifications, 36, 37,
    38–9
Country Programmable Aid
    (CPA), 31–2

debt cancellation, 7
decentralisation, 80
Democratic Republic of
    Congo, 49
Denmark, 5
deportees, 10–11
developed countries, 37
    see also donors
developing countries,
    2–3, 7–9
    see also recipient countries
    net financial flows to, 8
    shifts in, 36–7

DOI: 10.1057/9781137397881.0015

CPSIA information can be obtained at www.ICGtesting.com
Printed in the USA
LVOW13*1435090514

385157LV00007B/114/P